How to use this handbook

Review the table of contents prior to any beauty or wellness service for important information or just to check out what's new.

■

Keep handy for quick reference at home for tips on styling and optimal maintenance, safety rules, keeping your own records when doing treatments at home, reviewing common problems, and unique gift ideas.

■

Bring this handbook with you to the salon for a reminder of salon policies, to remind you of questions or concerns you may have, and to journal your stylist's tips & instructions.

■

Take this book with you on trips for tips while traveling, pampering ideas while on vacation, or to journal possible new techniques or formulas that might be used in a different salon.

Table of Contents

YOUR NO-NONSENSE GUIDE TO *Salon & Spa* SERVICES

What
You
Should
Know
Before
You
Go

The information in this book is true and complete to the best of our knowledge. All recommendations are made without guarantee on the part of the author or Education In Motion. The author and publisher disclaim any liability incurred with the use of this information.

Published by **E**m Education In Motion
Cover design by Lisa Kirkpatrick

Printed in the United States

Franklin Press
Baton Rouge, LA

For orders, questions or comments contact us at:
Education In Motion
5700 Berkshire Avenue
Baton Rouge, LA 70806

salontips@earthlink.net

1

SERVICE OPTIONS

Even permanent waves aren't ever *really* permanent since, fortunately or unfortunately, hair grows! However, the idea of drastic, unwanted change makes even the most daring client cringe! Even very temporary changes such as make-up for a special occasion can be time-consuming disappointments. Obviously, and more serious, is any misguided application or procedure which either damages the hair or skin or has long-term consequences. Therefore, knowing *what* you want and what your options are is essential. This knowledge can also make the entire salon or spa experience that much more pleasant as well as help you to get what you want. Listed in the pages to come--under general subject headings--are the most common salon and spa services available. And since there are many more services offered with new ideas springing up every day, the following is only the beginning of what's out there regarding **the latest in beautification, preservation, and wellness**.

Who Does What?

In some salon situations, a client may well have a half dozen or so people working with her even though she has a scheduled appointment with only one person. For example, the client is first addressed by the receptionist who is there to greet her, to answer questions, and sometimes to escort and direct her to prepare for service. From then on, the client may encounter a variety of helpers or assistants who instruct her to change into a smock, offer her a beverage, shampoo or blow-dry her hair (if she is having her hair done), or either initiate or complete a skin care or chemical procedure. This causes some clients concern if they prefer or expect to have one person manage their entire service--which does occur in many salons. But by the time your appointment arrives, your stylist may have already scheduled appointments too closely together to accommodate your every need. Also keep in mind that some stylists or technicians *always* only provide one service, so arrangements may have to be made even just to blow-dry your hair after, for example, a coloring service.

<u>Best Advice</u>: As with all of your questions or concerns, address them when you make your appointment.

What's New - Extra! Extra!

Hair analysis, computer imaging, scalp treatments, and blow-dry or make-up lessons are just a few of the common and more accessible extras that have been around for a while. Image consulting, wardrobe consulting, and personal shopping are also becoming mainstay services among today's active clientele. For fun and flash, a number of "style & shoot" salons have also popped up. Here, individuals or entire parties can dress up in one of many outfits provided by the salon, get a new style and make-up, and then have a photo session all in one place.

There is, however, an even longer list of *new* services provided today by salons and spas. Body-healing therapies, fitness training, cranial massage, accupressure, exfoliating scrubs, light therapy, herbal or seaweed wraps, cellulite treatments, aromatherapy treatments, and reflexology, are just a few. Also gaining popularity are such services as 10 stress-reducing minutes in a steam tube pumped with fragrance and music, massaging tables and beds complete with CDs to choose from for listening through the attached headphones, or a sensory deprivation tank with built-in video screen playing nature scenes while you float peacefully buoyant in warm water. And if that weren't enough, extras like Mendi Body Art, tattooing, dreadlocks, crochet braids, and a variety of weaves are gaining momentum in more urban areas and near student campuses. If nutritional counseling or health-oriented services are what you're after, many spas have a referral list of consultants who are either on call or available for appointments outside the salon.

Many spas also now provide a number of different detoxification treatments to flush out the body's toxins and impurities. Some detox programs even give homework that include herbal drinks, fasting, and follow-up. What's more? **There are now products that can fix hair and skin** by actually improving it *or* giving the illusion that it's improved! New polymers calm down frizziness and add shine to hair; purifying products remove build-up and residues due to other products or the environment; and natural or synthetic adhesives repair beaten hair and torn nails. There's even a

2

whole new way of looking at salon chemicals, too! How do you find what you're looking for? See **Know your resources** on p. 56 in **SALONS**.

Did you know? The latest in salon practices include displays for local designers' jewelry, clothing, and art to be sold on consignment in addition to a wide array of gift items for purchase.

Consultants

Whether you need color consulting, wardrobe consulting, or image consulting, many salons and spas have access to these experts who provide services "on call" or by separate appointments outside the salon or spa. If it has to do with beauty or fashion, chances are your receptionist or stylist can point you in the right direction. Personal shoppers and closet organizers can also be sought through a salon or spa. In addition, consultants can also cross-reference other consultants.

Layered

Cropped

Bobbed

Clippered

Razored

Texturized

Thinned

Shaped

Trimmed

Haircuts

It can all be quite confusing. To prove this point let us examine the meanings of short and long hair:
Short hair can be described as: Short all over (military short), short all over above the shoulders, short in one area only (e.g., layered on top), or short around the perimeter of the head but longer through the interior lengths.

Long hair can be described as: One-length or layered, from shoulder length down to the middle of one's back or longer, or short around the perimeter but longer all through the top (just as mentioned above.)
These definitions, of course, depend on what you or your stylist consider to be short or long, and should be

discussed in detail before the service begins. And if that weren't complicated enough, the variations in-between are endless. There are classic cuts, trendy cuts, precision cuts, romantic cuts, and the latest cuts, and that's just the beginning!

How do you know what's right for you? Bring your ideas to your stylist by being prepared for your consultation. Examples include things you like, things you don't like, and what worked and didn't work in the past. Also take some time to consider how much time you have or *want* to work on your hair. Regarding a particular look, questions pertaining to maintenance--while at home or how often you should return to the salon--will help you and your stylist come up with the perfect look. Just want a trim for more of the same look? Be sure to go over all the details again anyway during the consultation even when seeing your usual stylist.
Better: Check out all the tips in the next chapter including Tips For Duplicating A Haircut You Like in **COMMUNICATING WITH YOUR STYLIST**, p. 34.

Did you know? Many have speculated as to the differences between the 15-minute haircut and the 60-minute haircut. Even the experts on both sides will argue whether or not spending more time, using finer sections, and cutting with more precision makes for a better haircut. Why the discrepancy? Training. And although it is true that the more highly trained stylists take the most time per service, more education doesn't always mean more experience. The decision is simple: How much time does it take for you to be happy?

Bad Hair Day?

If your hair is never just quite right or just harder to work with than usual on a particular day, it could be due to any of the following reasons:

- something you are or are not doing connected with styling, products, or physical manipulations to the hair
- stress or illness
- medication or diet

4

- changes in your environment (air pollution, high or low humidity, your tap water)
- grown out conditions (out of shape cut, perm, or color)

Your stylist will be happy to talk with you about your "bad hair days" so that together you can find an answer.

Hair Styling

Whether you are after some elaborate "do" for a special occasion, fancy braids or dreadlocks, or a simple set with rollers, try to use as many descriptive words as you can in conveying your desired result. Romantic, carefree, wild, messy, controlled, sophisticated, or fun, are just some of the adjectives that conjure up a kind of *style* in our minds. Up or down? Loose or tight? Wrapped with ribbons or beads? There are so many different "dos" that if you don't know what something is called, use the tips suggested in The Good Client on p. 32 in **COMMUNICATING WITH YOUR STYLIST**. Best Advice: Ask your stylist to show you his styling books, magazines or portfolio for some ideas. If you don't have any preconceived ideas, he can probably make the best suggestion of all if you'll let him! F.Y.I: Be aware that some hairstyles--depending on the technique--take several hours while other jobs take only minutes.

Hairdos For Special Occasions

If the look you desire for a wedding or gala is important to you, don't leave it to the last minute. Even though you want your hair done just prior to the special event, it is strongly advised that you have at least a consultation with your stylist or a trial appointment on a prior date--especially if you're seeing a stylist for the first time. Sometimes, a stylist will offer a discount for the trial appointment if she doesn't need an entire appointment time for this "try-out" session to see your hair, look at pictures, or just talk over different ideas. **Sometimes this consultation appointment will be FREE**.

But even if you do have to spend extra money to make sure you and your hairstylist are speaking the same language on the special look and style, it's better than waiting until the day of your important occasion to discover you don't like the hairstyle at all! Need another reason? The trial appointment

5

or lengthy consultation is also a great time to bring any items you'd like to use for hair ornaments such as a veil, headpiece, ribbons, flowers, or hat. Pictures, swatches, or material from your apparel (if accessible) will also be of help to your stylist for ideas. Tip: You and your stylist may have a wonderful relationship, but if she admits she doesn't do a lot of gala and party hair or "up-dos", don't frustrate both of you just because you don't want anyone else to touch your locks. Instead, ask your stylist to suggest a competent colleague to provide just that one service, and you'll all be happier.

Did you know? Hairstylists (as well as make-up artists) will frequently meet you and your party at another location outside the salon for an additional fee. This is an especially popular idea for weddings and family photo shoots. Hair and make-up can also be provided for other members of your party as long as the requests are relatively simple for the stylist or make-up artist. Hint: Schedule this type of service far in advance!

Flattering Cuts & Styles For You

Should you avoid chin-length cuts if you have a round face? Is short hair best if you're petite? In most cases, the answer to these questions is yes. However, although every salon carries books which list the "rules" and depict the perfect style for your facial shape, there are so many more factors that stylists must take into consideration when approaching your cut or style. Body shape, lifestyle, and sometimes age may play a factor. Other basic ideas include emphasizing your positive features and minimizing the negative ones, but even the best ideas will fall short if the canvas is not appropriate. In other words, hair that is extremely thick or extremely thin has its limitations. The same goes for super fine or super coarse hair. The answer? Discuss these issues with your stylist in detail in addition to seeing some hair books if there is time. Better: Have a look at some books or magazines ahead of time on your own or arrive at the salon early. (Also see Using Pictures in **COMMUNICATING WITH YOUR STYLIST**, p. 27.)

Average costs of haircuts and styles? Haircuts and hair styling services have the widest price range of all the salon services. Because stylists can charge as little as $6 or as much as $100 or more with everything in-between, even an average of $45 is not really accurate. Why the range? Like other types of artists, many stylists can make their own prices based on their education, skill, demographics, or the degree of pampering service you are likely to experience as compared with their competitors. Also, like retailers, stylists prices reflect supply and demand. F.Y.I: "Hairdos" for special occasions may cost more than a stylist's usual styling fee. Don't forget to expect extra if booking an on-location service.

Single process:

temporary,

semi-permanent,

demi-permanent,

permanent

Touch-ups

High / low lighting

Bleach & tone

Creative color

Corrective color

Hair Color

How light? How dark? How *colorful*? Before you can research your options with hair color, think about and answer the following questions: Do you want your hair colored all over? Would you like it to be as permanent (or temporary) as possible? Would you prefer highlights of one or many colors? Flashy, noticeable color? Or as subtle and natural-looking as possible? Hair colorists can temporarily color the hair's surface layer, permanently alter the hair's pigmentation and composition, or apply color that fades away over time. Although some color processes are chemical, **many natural and botanical products are used to color hair.** Factors that colorists take into consideration include permanency, maintenance issues for the client, suitability and most importantly--feasibility. Factors that the client must consider include desired degree of change, depth, intensity, brightness, and gray coverage.

Producing specific shades and tones has more to do with science, but a colorist's application techniques are individually creative. In addition, first-time hair color clients benefit from having their options and color procedures explained ahead of time when seeing an experienced professional instead of attempting it themselves at home. Once feasibility is established, nuances of tone and hue can be customized. Questions you may care to ask of a technician include: Will it require a maintenance program? Will tints or bleach be used? What is the difference? What is the lasting or fading time? You can understand more about your options when your colorist explains which type of hair color is best for you and why. Note: Be careful not to expect miracles from your technician when you have a head full of existing chemicals, brittle or damaged hair, or--as your colorist may explain-- when you have a naturally complex situation. Even the best stylists cannot control every factor. (For a lot more on hair coloring, see **COLORING, PERMING, AND OTHER TREATMENTS AT HOME**, beginning on p. 80.)

WARNING! A patch-test (allergy test for hair color) is advised but not usually performed in the salon prior to a new hair color service. If you suspect you might be allergic or simply want to test your reaction to a particular product, it will be up to you to request to have a test the day before your scheduled appointment. How is it done? A small amount of the color mixture will be applied to an area, usually on the arm. Allergic reactions are revealed within 24 hours.

Flattering Hair Color For You

Should you go lighter as you get older? Can gray hair be shaded blonde while leaving the rest of the hair its natural color? In most cases, the answer to these questions is yes, but there's a whole lot more that goes into considering the most flattering hair color for you. Even with subtle color, the stylist must visualize where to strategically place the highlights--taking all factors into consideration before she approaches you with a bottle or brush. Lifestyle, age, hair type, and skin tone are just a few of these factors--creating distinctly different approaches to each individual client. In the case of many hair color options, maintenance is also going to be an issue for some clients--with some looks requiring monthly maintenance and some requiring much less. It is wise to see the books available in your stylist's salon depicting various colorful looks. The hair color swatches your colorist can show you will also give you some idea of color shades and tones. The best idea when it comes to the right hair color for you? Communicate, communicate, communicate.

Did you know? Your make-up *and* wardrobe colors may need slight or drastic adjustment when changing your hair color. If your colorist does not mention your *"cool"* (blues, charcoals, pinks) make-up being out of balance with your new *"warm"* (copper-reds, golden) hair color, take it upon yourself to consult a make-up artist and possibly a general color consultant. Your salon will be happy to refer you or help you locate either professional.

Corrections For Color (& Perms)

Maybe you've paid for a botched job. Maybe you did it yourself. Perhaps the disastrous state of your hair--due to a chemical treatment--was an unforeseen accident by an otherwise competent stylist. All you know is that you have to do something. That something is a correction.

Few stylists will argue that chemical correction is a specialty requiring the proper education and experience. In fact, these days, more stylists are willing to "pass the buck" and refer a client to a colleague (or outside their salon if necessary) with a particular type of experience rather than struggle with a difficult situation with which they may not be as familiar. Dentists don't perform heart surgery, and it's no longer expected that one stylist be good at everything with such a wide range of specialized talents in the various disciplines of the salon industry today. Unfortunately, correction is usually expensive as well as tricky. Worried about paying twice? Each salon or individual stylist will have their own policies regarding correction fees. If you return to a stylist who made an error in judgment, you may be entitled to one or more free services. (See Just Not Happy in **COMMUNICATING WITH YOUR STYLIST**, p. 36.) If there was simply a breakdown in communication, the correction or adjustment may only be discounted. It is therefore advised to allow the stylist who initially performed the service to perform a "re-do" whenever possible--an option lost to those making mistakes with at-home kits. If, however, you'd care not to return to the same stylist for a correction, request a refund to ease the high cost of seeing another technician. Most importantly, when requiring a correction, remember this: **What cannot be fixed or altered, can only be cut**. Make no mistake. If cutting your hair is not an option, growing out hair that is severely damaged or distasteful with only an occasional trim may turn out to be a very long and frustrating alternative.

Did you know? Sometimes the best advice from a color or perm specialist is to do *nothing* to correct a bad hair problem and wait instead for the hair to grow out, change, or get cut off eventually. Sometimes, however, the application of more chemicals can *appear* to fix problems caused by the initial chemicals. Best Advice? Seek more than one FREE corrections consultation before deciding the best approach.

Average costs of hair color services? Single process color (tint retouches and most semi- and demi-permanent applications) could cost you anywhere from $25 to $50 on average. The range for highlighting is wider depending on how much of the head is to be highlighted, the time it takes the stylist, and what technique is used. Long-haired or complex highlighting could cost upwards of $125, but this type of natural-looking color application is performed much less frequently than the once-a-month single process color or touch-up. Other specialty color applications--from bleach & tones to creative and corrective color--require such a subjective approach that no average cost can be given.

Why Color And Perm?

- It can make problem-to-style hair easier to manage.
- It can help you grow out, or better cope with problems from previous chemicals.
- Creative color and perms can enhance individuality.
- Color adds depth and luster creating the appearance of healthier hair.
- Perms can redirect inconsistent natural curl or wave.
- Relaxing makes hair smoother, slicker, and shinier.
- New techniques are quick and inexpensive.
- Change can be fun!

When To Color, When To Perm

If you plan to have both a permanent wave and permanent tint on your hair at the same time, note the following: If you're starting out virgin (no chemicals presently on the hair) or only have a non-metallic semi-permanent color, **perm first, then color**. If you already have permanent hair color all over, **retouch your color first, then perm**. Unless otherwise instructed by your stylist, you should perm hair that is all the same composition whenever possible. In other words, if you're going to color your regrowth anyway, better to do it a week or so before you perm, so the curl or wave will be the same consistency all the way through. Why? Tinted hair "takes" the perm solution in half the time and cannot be left on longer just to process the slow virgin outgrowth.
F.Y.I: Unfortunately, you'll have to freshen up your permanent color due to the fading that occurs as a result of perming.

DANGER!! By not telling your stylist exactly what chemical properties are present on your hair at the time of service, you are taking a chance that the next chemical being applied could have disastrous results.

Perming:

partial

root

spot

creative

re-directive

Perms & Relaxers

Soft and wavy? Wildly curly? Silky and straight? So many decisions to make. The biggest factors in determining the kind of "loop"? Rod size and type of perm solution. The type of solution used is also important for hair straightening--which is usually combed through the hair or gently worked through with gloved fingers. Yet another technique? Curls can be softened with relaxing cream first and then wrapped around perm rods to re-curl the hair. Knowing how you want your hair to look is the easy part--getting it is the trick! In other words, how the hair will "take" the applied chemical requires a professional, educated guess, and the most favorable results are possible when each variable is considered and handled properly. The variables? Hair texture, porosity, virginity (or hair's lack of virginity), density, length, and elasticity, along with tools used, procedures, rod application, and solutions, combine to produce a variety of outcomes.

Whether you want a designer perm, soft wave, or stick-straight hair, allow your stylist to explain which perm or relaxer is best for you and why. You may also want to discuss maintenance of your look. Perming repeatedly is not advised to avoid perming over (and possibly damaging) previously permed hair. Many technicians, however, use special techniques to perm the re-growth only. <u>Tip</u>: Trimming hair that has been permed at least every 4-6 weeks can make a perm appear to last longer and look bouncier. Why? The acquired length due to growing hair can weigh a perm down significantly. As the style is reformed and the weight alleviated, the perm bounces back! (For a lot more on perming and relaxing, see **COLORING, PERMING & OTHER TREATMENTS AT HOME**, beginning on p. 80.)

Relaxing:

virgin

touch-up

relax & curl

spot

corrective

12

Did you know? Your technician may suggest not shampooing 1-2 days prior to applying certain chemicals to your hair. The idea is not to scrub the scalp beforehand so that natural oils secreted from your scalp can act as a barrier creating less irritation on the scalp during processing. If your stylist doesn't suggest it, ask.

Average costs of perms & relaxers? At first glance, perms and relaxers look like the most expensive service on the salon menu. Virgin relaxers average $60 with touch-ups costing just a bit less. Perms to curl average between $65 -$85 and may not include the haircut. Certainly, these services can be gotten for less, but can cost much more depending on your location. Why so costly? All perms must endure a series of specific procedures before, during, and after the directive technique or rod placement--taking up more appointment time than many other services. Even just perming or relaxing the virgin outgrowth for touch-up service requires the same calculated, step-by-step procedures for optimal results, and may cost only slightly less than the initial service. Fortunately, perms and relaxers can look good for several months (despite inevitable new growth) and, in some cases, until the hair is completely cut off.

Manicures:

basic,

french,

designer

Pedicures

Artificial nails

Nail repair

Nail Services

Most manicurists have a complete menu with services and prices available for review at their stations or tables, but seldom are all the options that are available fully explained on paper. Nail care is becoming more and more popular as well as artistic with a variety of services to choose from. Many men also see the value in manicured looking hands and nails and opt for "no polish" service-- enjoying all but the color. If it's pampered feet you're after, pedicures are relaxing, beautifying, and inexpensive services for men and women, and make great gifts, too! Hand, arm, and foot massages with paraffin treatments are also usually available for that extra soaking and soothing skin care.

Many manicurists are also trained in the art of reflexology-- massaging pressure points in the hands or feet to balance organs within the body. What else can a manicurist do for you? Maybe you'd like to know about the fun decals or latest fashion colors available. Perhaps she can even do your nails while you're getting your hair done. Other questions you might ask? Does a lengthy foot massage come with the price of a basic pedicure? Does she trim or just push back the nail cuticle? What is her approach to the various types of artificial nails and their maintenance? See the nail expert--the manicurist--for the answer to these and other questions. Remember: Many manicurists sell dozens of colors of nail polish in addition to tools and products for complete nail care, nail strengthening and growth products. Tip: Since most of us are hard on our hands, be sure to get your manicurist's expert advice on proper hand and nail care before you leave her chair.

Artificial Nails

If you want more beautiful, stronger, or longer nails than you can achieve naturally, consider artificial nails. The most common types are acrylic, silk, and fiberglass. Whether you want extensions or "overlays" (adding one of these materials to strengthen your own nails without the extension), **the technique and material used depends on your needs and your manicurist's preference**. For example, acrylic may provide the strongest nail tip, but can be harder on natural nail beds than the alternatives. If silk or fiberglass material is used, the thinner, more pliable nail may look more natural and be easier to remove, but will also tend to be less durable. Whichever substance your manicurist chooses, "filling" the nail with more of that substance for durability can mean bi-weekly visits--not to mention the occasional repair; therefore, the cost of maintenance should be considered. Additionally, once you've committed to acrylic, silk, or fiberglass nails, removal of the artificial nail is sometimes arduous. An easier, temporary solution? Less natural-looking plastic nail tips. F.Y.I: Sometimes the material used is not as important as *how well* it is used. Note: Ask your manicurist about her replacement or patch policy on broken or chipped artificial nails. It is sometimes FREE, or very inexpensive.

Did you know? Climate plays a role in how well nail products and procedures will work for you. For example, a more humid climate makes using gel products for artificial nails nearly impossible.

Average costs of nail services? Basic manicures average a reasonable $12-$18 for a 30 minute indulgence--with "French" and designer manicures costing a bit extra. Pedicures average around $30 for feet pampering, and a deluxe treatment with soothing paraffin for hands or feet costs a bit more. Artificial nails cost more for the initial full set (around $50), and then "fills" to maintain most types of artificial nails run about $25 on average. And as mentioned earlier, to patch, repair, or replace a nail tip is either free or as little as $5.

Hair removal

Lash tinting

Facials

Acid peels

Back cleansing

Impurities
    extractions

Glandular
    stimulation

Tanning

Make-up

Skin Care Services

Aesthetics, as defined by Webster's, is "a branch of philosophy dealing with beauty and the beautiful," and this is the basis of the aesthetician's (or skin care specialist's) work. With so many skin "care" services and products out there, it is virtually impossible to know what is used for what and when, or why there are so many services and products to begin with; but any aesthetician is happy to give you a complete guide to the services and products she provides and endorses. What she needs to know from you is what you need and want-- having already given some thought to the following questions: Do you want your skin "care" for prevention of aging, dry or oily skin? Would you like to know more about skin care services for relaxation purposes only? Would you like care for healthy maintenance or a change in appearance? Would you like alternatives to medication or surgery to treat skin problems? Keep in mind that your aesthetician will not hesitate in advising you to seek the help of a dermatologist or even a cosmetic surgeon should basic beautifying treatments not do the job.

But take comfort in knowing that **certain products and therapies provided by an aesthetician *can* sometimes prevent skin problems from getting worse**--or from becoming a problem to begin with--sometimes eliminating the need for a physician. Benefits may include minimizing the signs of aging, a smoother, more radiant complexion, and refined pores. Facials with accompanying massages can increase circulation or even assist in treatment of overactive glands. Some doctors even treat acne with the help of an aesthetician. Steam treatments and impurities extractions (removal of dead cells)--when done correctly with proper at-home maintenance--can leave skin looking like a baby's bottom, and aid in long-lasting, healthy, skin. Even regular eye-lift treatments can eliminate the need for cosmetic surgery. In addition, skin resurfacing has come a long way with the use of new and improved botanical or chemical acid peels and alpha-hydroxy acids. New technology also allows the aesthetician to use special machinery made to either detect skin damage or even cause change--such as impairing or stimulating hair growth. (Also see **ALERT!** later in this chapter.)

As we see in the other disciplines, each individual technician will prefer products and techniques with which she is familiar, and she probably has something just right for you. Important tips: **1)** check the credentials of those who prescribe pharmaceuticals or use invasive techniques, **2)** get more than one consultation, **3)** speak to former clients or patients, and **4)** ask about cases of infection, scarring, and allergies related to products or procedures. F.Y.I: Aestheticians and make-up artists are also almost always specialists in their particular fields, but there are some services--such as eyebrow shaping--which can be provided by either technician. Massage is also sometimes provided by aestheticians, but in most states an aesthetician's license only allows massage to be performed on specific areas of the body--mostly the face, neck, and shoulder region.

Skin care services of interest to the average client? Before glancing over the list of skin care services provided below, there are still more questions to ponder: Does an invigorating aromatherapy bath or skin rejuvenating treatment interest you? Have you considered temporary or permanent hair removal? As with certain hair, nail, and massage services--depending on the desired result--there may be an emphasis on upkeep, so keep in mind whether the services are geared towards appearance or preservation.

ALERT!! Although laser treatment can be safer and less painful than some other hair removal techniques, it is a procedure which should only be performed by a certified professional. Should you decide to have it done in a salon, talk with your physician first. In addition, permanent hair removal, regardless of the technique, cannot be 100% guaranteed.

Did you know? Red, inflamed, or flaking skin is a common but temporary condition immediately following certain skin care treatments. (Also see What You Must Always Tell Your Stylist in **COMMUNICATING WITH YOUR STYLIST**, p. 35.) The climate in which you live also plays a role in which products and procedures will work best for you.

Tanning

There is nothing quite like having rosy, healthy-looking cheeks, or a beautifully bronzed body--looking as if you're fresh from a day at the beach. And now, tanning salons have created the mood complete with stereos, fans, and fragrant lotions. The bad news? **There is no such thing as healthy tan!** Although a little color may make you *look* healthier, tanning of any kind is still not good for your skin--especially when overexposed. In other words, you're not likely to find a dermatologist who'll give you the thumbs up on even the latest technology in tanning. If you must tan, check to make sure the bed you use is a new model and appears to be in good working order. Also check to see that the salon will only allow you to tan within the safest guidelines--usually only 20 minutes at a time. Good advice? If you must use tanning beds don't overdo it.

The best news yet? You can now get a natural-looking tan from tanning creams and lotions. These are safe, topical dyes that "take" a few hours after being applied. Whether you want a hint of color or a rich, dark tan, you can find just the right shade to compliment your skin tone. They are available at cosmetic counters everywhere for self-application, but you can also have tanning cream thoroughly applied by an aesthetician. Ask for a **Self-Tanner with Exfoliation**. First, old skin is sloughed off with an invigorating massage (this maximizes the creams potential), and then the cream is applied in all the major visible areas. How long does the tan last? About the same as a natural tan--from a few days to a week--fading gradually. The salon that offers this service will also sell the tanning cream separately to do yourself at home. Tip: If you have it applied at the salon and there is tanning cream leftover, ask to take the rest of it home.

Did you know? Not only are tanning creams the safest way to look sun-kissed, most of them have 15 SPF or more protection--fooling everyone including the sun!

ALERT! Pills that bring on tanned-looking skin darken your entire body--even your eyelids and the palms of your hands. As with any medication, consult your doctor or a dermatologist before deciding if these pills are right for you.

Make-Up

Sometimes also extremely knowledgeable about skin care, a salon make-up artist is able to do more than apply pretty colors to your face. She can reshape your eyebrows, smooth away lines and circles with the stroke of a brush, or create a look to complement a new you. Can't do it yourself? Let her *teach you* how to keep up the new look at home. Many artists also travel to do make-up on location for special occasions like weddings and photo shoots, and may be as masterful at "natural looking" make-up as transforming your look. But make-up artists have their specialties, too. Theater make-up artists work very differently from salon make-up artists who service clients for a daily look; and the professional you want to hire for a photo shoot should have photography make-up training or experience. Whether applying make-up, providing make-up instruction, or improving your appearance with corrective techniques, **skillfully applied make-up can bring about the most improved change in your appearance**.

When should you change your make-up? When your hair color has changed in any way--naturally or with products--or when you're changing your wardrobe colors. Be sure to look the way you normally do on a daily basis when you go in for your appointment, and talk to a make-up artist about the colors you normally like to wear. Most importantly, be sure to let her know how much time you are *willing* to spend applying your make-up in the morning. Tip: Sometimes you can even bring in your own stockpile of make-up when having a make-up "lesson." And, who knows, you may already have everything you need except the techniques!

Average costs of skin care services? Facials can incorporate various products or techniques for the purpose of deep cleansing, treating problematic skin, or simple relaxation. The cost ranges anywhere from $25 to $75. The time allotted for treatment also accounts for some of the cost. Quick services such as lash or brow tinting or shaping cost around $10-$20. Hair removal costs range from a few dollars for lip or chin waxing to more than $500 for a treatment that uses special machinery. The average bikini wax? Around $20. If you join a monthly membership program for tanning, each individual session will average $1-5 for a typical 20-minute session, but it takes about 5 sessions to bronze your body. Self-tanning applications are available in your high-end salons, costing around $75 to exfoliate the skin and then apply the tanning cream. Make-up applications start at around $25. Add a worthwhile $15-$20 for technique instruction, and remember that on-location service is additional.

Massage Services

Would you prefer a relaxing or energizing massage? One to relieve stress or pain? How about just for fun? Whether your massage therapist is trained in Swedish or Shiatsu therapy, Rolfing or Reiki, or combining your massage with accupressure, a basic understanding of your therapist's specialized technique is necessary information before scheduling an appointment. These masters of touch can either gently take away the tensions of one bad day, or arrange a personalized program of treatments with long-term benefits. Also keep in mind that there are many different types of masseurs and therapies to choose from. To ease pain from an aching body, injury, or misalignment, some massaging techniques may involve some rough or slightly uncomfortable manipulations, so it is important to seek out the right kind of massage for a special need. When focused on certain areas, massage can stimulate and strengthen muscle fibers and body tissues. Some techniques are designed for structural alignment--improving posture and health, and **in some cases, massages can even prevent future health problems or pain**.

In fact, more and more massage therapists work in hospitals today collaborating with physicians. Some "body healers" use holistic methods or therapies incorporating ancient eastern philosophy. Others are teachers of massage--teaching parents how to massage their infants, or couples how to massage one another. Massages can be had singly or as part of a series of treatments, depending on the goal and technique. "Symphony" massages--two therapists who massage one client at the same time--are also available at some day spas. As stated in the chapter titled **STYLISTS** on p. 73, not all massage therapists are required to take a state board exam, but most fulfill the necessary training and certification needed for the specific massages they provide. Other therapists who have apprenticed but have no certification might be just as good; as suggested when seeking any "hands-on" service provider, inquire about his experience and philosophy and ask him to explain what he will do before he begins. <u>Tip</u>: Basic, relaxing massages given by interns from the local massage therapy school are a great deal if your schedule is flexible. <u>F.Y.I</u>: Depending on the technique, clients are massaged partially or fully clothed (fully clothed with seated massages), or in the nude--covered with a sheet. Modest? Be sure to let your therapist know your preference.

Where can you get a massage? Spas and some hair salons, health/athletic clubs, sports centers and tanning salons, will either offer massage on location or refer you to a local therapist on whom you can call for a later appointment. For a small fee, many therapists will even bring a massage table or chair to your home. You can also find therapists doing seated massage and reflexology almost anywhere--including department and health food stores, an airport concourse, or even at the beach!

Did you know? Since many massage therapists work as independent contractors, their environments can be as unique as their techniques. One might burn incense, one might play music or nature sounds, and another might light the room with candles or colored light bulbs. Some massages are even given on the floor!

Average costs of massage services? The average fee for a quick seated massage is usually around $1 per minute. For basic table massages, the average cost ranges from $25 to $75--depending on the amount of time you schedule to be massaged. Most therapists schedule 30, 60 and 90 minute appointment times--with the longest time averaging less cost per minute. Specialized work or work that requires a series of visits typically costs more.

Not Just, But Especially For Men

Men are included in every aspect of this guide and are encouraged to seek out every preserving and pampering service that women enjoy. There are, however, services that pertain more to men than women despite the fact that many men don't take the time to research their service options.

What do men really want? Efficient, expeditious, convenient, quality service. Still, more and more men are enjoying the "extras" and discovering that it suits them to take advantage of salon and spa services. The reason? **When men take the time to look and *feel* better, the result is a feeling of well-being that carries over into their business and personal lives**. Whether he prefers a "sports" salon where he can simultaneously watch his favorite team, a sophisticated salon or barber shop where he gets a shoe shine at the same time as a haircut, or has his hair or nails done by a stylist who makes "corporate calls" to his office, the choice is his to make. The bottom line? Most men can do without the frills, but there are a number of quick, no-nonsense, inexpensive services that would appeal to many men if only they knew what was waiting for them.

Men's Hair Care

Hair care for men has come a long way since the ol' time barber shops, but what worked back then is making a comeback in a new way. And although barbers specialize in men's hair care, many cosmetologists study precision cuts for men with the same intensity since more women are sporting the same haircuts. **Do better cuts have to cost more?** Sometimes. But the key factors for a good, basic, short or long man's haircut are **a)** a stylist who does a lot of mens' haircuts, **b)** a cut or style that requires little or no at-home care, and **c)** regular trims every 4 to 6 weeks.
Tip: Ungroomed beards and mustaches, neck hair and hair growing from the ears, nose, and eyebrows can make men look more unkempt than an overgrown haircut. F.Y.I: For easier beard and mustache trimming at home, invest in a good trimmer--especially for that purpose--available at beauty supply and some drug stores. (Only a stylist, however, knows how to design facial hair to camouflage the gaps.)

When it comes to coloring and perming, most men prefer a natural look, whereas women are more willing to have *designed* color or curl--even when the style looks intentional. Popular "at-home color" kits for men consists of either natural stains or metallic, inorganic dyes that gradually cover gray by adding color cumulatively. (See Hair Coloring At Home in **COLORING, PERMING, & OTHER TREATMENTS AT HOME**, p. 81.) For the most natural looks--including the most natural-looking camouflage for gray hair--it is wise to consult with a colorist first. She can add subtle "sun streaks" with highlights that require little or no maintenance, create a color plan that can be maintained at home, and can even provide a natural-looking wave to give thinning hair some kick.

ATTENTION MEN! Note the tips on p. 30 for better service.

Men's Skin & Nail Care

Nostalgia and a great gift idea aren't the only reason a good shave and hot compresses are making a comeback. Many men have also discovered what women have known for years, which is that **a combination of indulgence and personal hygiene is one of the best ways to relieve stress**. Not only can a man benefit from a deep pore facial or exfoliating scrub just as much as a woman, but he can enjoy it, too! And what good are an expensive watch or ring and stylish cufflinks without refined looking hands and nails? And if you're a "mister fix-it" on the weekends, don't think your colleagues won't notice! Fortunately, it's nothing that a "no-polish" 20 to 30 minute manicure can't take care of just in time for that big meeting. A totally relaxing massage and hot tub soak isn't a bad idea either--especially after that long, hard day. So why is the average man less likely to pamper than are his women friends? Golf or television may still be that man's preferred way to relax, so it might be up to his friends or partner to help him realize that there's an entirely new way to look better, feel better, and relieve stress. And for some, the only way to get him in that salon or spa is to make the appointment and take him there.

Did you know? The latest trend in full-service for men is providing an environment where men can do business while their salon needs are attended to--all in one place. Since men frequently complain that there just isn't enough time in the day, these new hot spots will allow him to bring his cell phone or lap top, watch the stock market, and get a haircut and shoe shine all at the same time!

Hair Loss & Your Options

Two-thirds of women will face some hair loss at some point in their lives, but more men tend to thin and lose more earlier in their lives. Still, hair loss of any kind can produce great anxiety for either sex. The good news? With over-the-counter products no longer requiring a prescription and new remedies showing some promise in hair growth stimulation, hair loss can be slowed significantly if treatment is begun as soon as thinning is apparent. There are several reasons for thinning or loss, but the most common cause, heredity, can be delayed with the products available. **Some hair can even be rejuvenated. Other products for hair loss can at least stunt the activity that causes thinning and more loss, thereby making it worthwhile for those who feel it is too late**. These products work best when used as part of an entire line of products which may include shampoos, conditioners, and fixatives.

Hair loss due to illness? If an individual experiences sudden hair loss due to trauma, diet, medications, or stress, rather than the unrelenting fate of heredity, he should see a doctor immediately. In addition, it should be noted that only doctors can prescribe pharmaceutical treatment. Barbers, cosmetologists and aestheticians, on the other hand, can provide professional product information and perform services such as scalp treatments which combine products and massage, further stimulating growth and slowing the process of hair loss. In addition, many men and women who have thinning hair swear by their salon hair color and curls for the *appearance* of thicker, fuller hair, without noticing more thinning or loss as a result. Note: As with any medicinal or chemical products, directions, disclaimers, and risks should be taken seriously.

Interested in information on wigs and hairpieces? See Wigs & Hair Pieces on p. 97 in **MORE STUFF**.

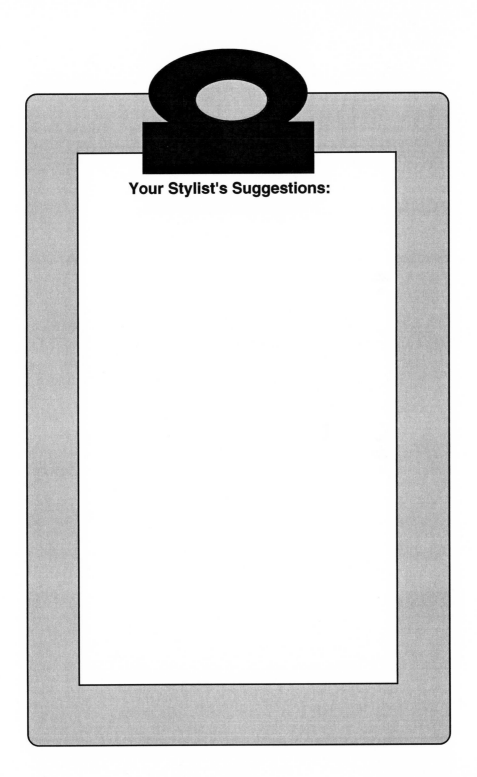

Your Stylist's Suggestions:

2
COMMUNICATING
WITH YOUR STYLIST

The Problem

As frustrating for the stylist, technician, or therapist as it is for the client, the inability to communicate successfully is the number one reason that clients end up dissatisfied. Not because it's all the client's fault, and not because it's all the service provider's fault; but because the services provided by salon professionals are so abstract that **terminology used by both the client and stylist conjures up different and personalized images**. The result? Both stylist and client are unaware that the other person has *not* understood what the end result will look or be like until it's (sometimes) too late. There is little protection against a provider who is incompetent, but the ideas in this chapter may help you see things from a different perspective and ultimately aid in achieving a more successful service.

Getting Closer To Your Goal

Even if you and your service provider are longtime friends and he knows you personally, your vacation plans and your kids' names, it is still your responsibility to remind him of 3 things each visit: **1)** what your needs and goals are, **2)** whether you want consistency or change, and **3)** what you liked and disliked about your last service.

To minimize frustration surrounding your service while preserving your client/stylist relationship, keep in mind the following steps that *you* as the client can take:

◇ **Communicate your ideas**. Be consistent in expressing your needs in the same fashion each visit instead of leaving the stylist to recall what he did the last time. If your goal or situation changes, be specific.

◇ **Listen carefully**. *Hear* your stylist when he says you simply can't have what you're asking for. Also pay special attention to problems, risks, or commitments regarding your request. Remember that just because something seems easy or feasible, it doesn't mean that it will work for or on you. Express your service desires, and then ask your stylist to explain in detail if, when, and how you can achieve the desired look.

◇ **Understand nature**. Since humans are not machines, an individual stylist's mood or inclination reflects his approach to the case at hand--which varies from one day to the next. For example, on the day of your appointment, if every client before you has requested subtle, natural-looking hair color, your colorist may approach your hair with more conservatism than the usual adventuresome approach you expect. And depending on the type of "hands-on" service, even the slightest change in position, pressure, or tension can alter the final result.

Did you know? The most common client complaint is that her stylist doesn't suggest or just do new and different things. Tip: Tell your stylist if that is what you expect. (Also see Consistency vs. Change later in this chapter.)

Using Pictures

The easiest way to convey an idea to your stylist that involves your appearance is with a picture or photograph. Pictures can be especially helpful for most haircuts, color and perms, make-up, nail shapes and colors, brow shaping, or anytime you need to be specific about a visual outcome. Fortunately or unfortunately, pictures from magazines tend to convey the most popular ideas at the time, so if you are interested in a classic look, it may require some searching for the right picture. Some stylists love pictures because in an instant they understand what the client pictures in her mind--saving everyone precious time. Even if the client is asking amiss, the stylist can begin the process of explaining possibilities and offering options if necessary. But sometimes **pictures can also be a source of frustration for the following reasons:**

• The model has a completely different hair or skin type, hair growth patterns, swirls or texture, a different face shape and features, or coloring. (Even if the same cut, techniques, or chemical processes are applied, the outcome will be different.)

- The model is bathed in strategic lighting, may have a ton of hair spray or other products on her hair or skin just for the photo shoot, may have a wind machine blowing her locks setting up a dramatic and unrealistic illusion of the hair, or her skin, coloring, and entire body are altered by digital computing.

- The client is looking at the face of the model rather than the hair adorning it or the make-up decorating the face. Tip: When using pictures of hairstyles, cover the face of the picture with your fingers just to be sure it's the hair that you're interested in so not to be distracted by the model's face.

What You Want vs. What You Have

Occasionally we look at someone we see on the street and say, "I'd like that hair (or skin)!" And much of the time, what we're admiring belongs to actors and models we see in print, television, and film. And because we tend to popularize the "beautiful people", we are often looking at actors and models that belong to the group of people who happen to have naturally great skin & hair! Unfortunately, in the real world, most of us have less than perfect bodies and less than perfect hair and skin. In fact, we can roughly estimate that 2% of the population has that perfect, flawless skin and that gorgeous, shiny, silky, "normal" hair that models seem to be blessed with. Their hair floats and bounces, catches the light just right, is easily colored and permed, and "behaves" when forced into anti-gravitational styles. The fact is, our culture is still caught up with unique bodily features, and those are the things that are most current and in style. It is not the norm. Day after day, stylists, aestheticians, and technicians are faced with the dreaded task of trying to communicate to their clients why they can't have the same look as the one sported by the model in the magazine picture. Best advice? Ask your stylist to explain how or why your hair or skin is different, and then be open to other suggestions if necessary.

Did you know? Personal trainers and nutritionists also run into the problem of trying to explain to their clients that due to genetics or their clients' natural conditions, their bodies may not look like ones they admire no matter how hard they work at it. Although this leads to great disappointment, the client should realize that **the best look is a look that balances every dimension and camouflages flaws.**

Consistency vs. Change

Consistency in service is actually more difficult to achieve than many people realize. Ever-changing external factors, a stylist's artistic mood, and a stylist's reliance on memory make it nearly impossible to get the *exact* same thing twice. There is really no such thing as a "factory line" haircut regardless of the technique, and even the exact mixing of product formulas will vary slightly from one service to the next. How do you get consistency in service? Once you've determined that you want to duplicate the service, make notes. **Your Stylist's Suggestions** at the end of each chapter and the **Sample Client Record** in the back of this handbook can be used. Also see Tips For Duplicating A Haircut You Like in **COMMUNICATING WITH YOUR STYLIST**, p. 34 for general tips that pertain to other services as well.

Some clients don't want the same thing twice. What they do want is **change.** This should not be a difficult request, but clients often tie the hands of their stylist at the same time they are asking for something new. For example, hair stylists frequently hear, "don't change the front, and leave the sides [like this], but give me *something* different." And since many haircutting, perming, make-up, hair removal, and highlighting techniques involve a type of "dot-to-dot" game, one step leads to another, and each change affects another change. Really ready for something new? Finding a picture from a salon book is helpful, but giving a trusted professional carte blanche may be the best idea yet!

What To Remember For A Successful Consultation

As the client, you cannot be expected to know a stylist's
artistic or technical abilities, terminology, educational
background or experience, but you can be proactive in
seeking a successful relationship with your stylist which
benefits you in the long run. And, **without useful tools of
your own, you might be headed for disaster even with the
most skilled of technicians standing before you**. For
example, when asking for "light" highlights to be woven
through your hair, if your colorist doesn't question your
meaning of "light", you may turn out with one of two distinctly
different results: either **1)** a head full of *subtly* colored
strands, or **2)** a heavy amount of very "light" blonde highlights
throughout. "Light" in this case means very different things.
Another example is asking for your hair to be cut "over" the
ears. That can also translate to one of two ideas: either
1) leaving hair *covering* the top of the ears, or **2)** cutting the
hair above the ear--*clearing* the ear of any hair.

So, although it should be the stylist's responsibility to help the
client communicate what he wants, it is also up to the client to
take charge lest he give up control with no concern for the
results. Even when the client/stylist relationship is friendly
and seems firmly established, frustration for both parties can
occur when the time is not taken to communicate needs and
desires. In other words, avoid miscommunication to avoid
long-term consequences or spoiled relationships. Without the
brief but critical interlude before service begins, you cannot be
certain that you and your stylist understand each other, and
even the most talented hands may not satisfy you.

Did you know? You can always request a quick
consultation each time you see your stylist--even if you are
a regular client. Remember to always let your stylist see
you as you normally appear for a realistic approach.

The Good Stylist

There are two simple phrases you can remember which will foster client/stylist communication during the most critical part of the service: The Consultation. Later in the chapter are some hints on being a good client, but how do you know you've found a good stylist? Remember the phrase "*A Lasting Professional Relationship*" or **A. L. P. R.** when assessing your stylist's consultation techniques, and the following will remind you what to look for.

A is for *Analyze*. The competent stylist will analyze your hair or skin before you even open your mouth. The hairstylist is examining your hair's texture, density, porosity, and elasticity, your general hair and scalp condition, and so on. He makes assessments as to how it will cut, color or perm depending on your requests. The aesthetician or make-up artist draws the same mental map regarding your skin's present state, the manicurist with your nails and hands, the massage therapist with your alignment and posture. The stylist or technician is also making a mental note of what will and won't work for you based on his experience. Unfortunately, you cannot know if your stylist is skilled in this silent act of reasoning, but you can tell if he is focused on you.

L is for *Listen*. The stylist should take a couple of minutes to listen to your requests, past problems, future goals, and anything else you think is important to mention. Keep in mind, however, that **the consultation cannot exceed the time needed to execute your service in the appointment time allowed**--usually completed anywhere from 30 minutes to an hour for haircuts, from one to several hours for chemical services, and anywhere from 30 to 90 minutes for various skin and nail care services. It is therefore suggested that you give some thought to what you want to say--even writing down ideas or questions--before you arrive for your appointment so you can be as brief and precise as possible. You want your stylist to hear what is pertinent. There is plenty of time to elaborate while the service is being rendered.

P is for *Possibilities*. A good stylist will gladly perform the service you desire whenever *possible*, but will offer advice or make suggestions if necessary. After all, you don't really want a service provided where there is a risk of danger or if there is a chance that what you've asked for simply won't work. Stylists should never just do what *they* want without

31

discussing their ideas with you, but as experts they may offer other--perhaps better--ideas for you. In fact, most people hope their stylist won't let them walk out with a look that is completely wrong for their hair, face, skin tone, or shape. The client knows what she likes on someone else, but usually wants her stylist to be honest if it'll be wrong for her.

R is for **Repeat**. This is actually the most crucial point of the consultation. You might think you've spent the last few minutes describing the exact color of red you had as a kid. A smart stylist will not only repeat back and confirm what you have said or what the two of you have agreed upon, but he will also give you examples of what he *understood* you to say--using key adjectives. This way, when your colorist verifies that you've asked for the kind of hair color similar to an Irish Setter, you will have an opportunity to confirm this example of copper-red or continue the conversation using other examples if he misunderstood.

The Good Client

Even though it is your stylist who is the professional and should take the lead in establishing or maintaining the client/stylist relationship, you are more likely to leave the salon happy by remembering the first letter of second phrase, **"Saving The Lasting Relationship"** or **S. T. L. R.** during your consultation with your stylist *before* service is to begin. You might even be saving yourself from a dissatisfying or disastrous service! **The client who can communicate her desires is a happy client!** The letters will remind you of the ideas listed below.

S is for **Show**. You may have nothing to show, but showing your stylist or technician something to convey what you want in addition to your verbal explanation can be a great time saver and help you to get what you want. A magazine picture or picture of yourself with a past "do" you liked (if it's a clear picture) is worth a thousand words--even though your stylist will need additional verbal information. Even obtaining a piece of real hair--past or present, yours or someone else's-- for hair color consultations can be tremendously helpful. For make-up appointments, bring in your own make-up to see what is working, not working, or missing in your collection. This also saves you from duplicating products that you already have. What else can you *show* your stylist? Use your own hands to mold, shorten, or cup your hair around your face as you describe your desired haircut, or use other stylists and clients in the salon as examples to relay what you like or don't like. Even, "her curl is nice, but I'd rather my perm be looser than that" is also more helpful than simply saying, "I'd like a body wave."

T is for ***Tell***. Tell your stylist what you have in mind in every way you know how, each and every visit, rather than assuming she speaks your *language*. Often the client assumes that his stylist knows what he means by a "short" cut, a "rich" color, or a "firm" massage. If you typically have trouble describing a visual result, think of a well-known celebrity ahead of time with whom to compare what you'd like or *not* like. Another tip is to describe what you want in sections. With a haircut for example, tell your stylist that at the front you'd like it [this short] while [*here*] at the back you'd like it left alone, and so on. You can even give specific measurements such as "1" on top." (For more, see Tips For Duplicating A Haircut You Like later in this chapter.)

L is for ***Listen***. *Listen* also shows up in the section on The Good Stylist (p. 31) because the stylist should really listen to your needs and desires. But be sure *you* listen to what the stylist tells you, too. Very often the client doesn't want to hear that she can't have her desired look or long-awaited service provided--regardless the reason. A client will argue that as a paying customer she should be able to get the service she has requested. The stylist therefore has to explain--as politely as possible--that **it isn't that she won't do the work, but that the work won't do!** So, make sure you really listen and understand what the stylist is going to do, can't do, or won't do.

R is for ***Repeat***. The plan, service agreement, or goal, needs to be confirmed by the stylist and the client just prior to beginning service. No matter that this seems redundant; better safe than sorry! This is also a good time to confirm what the total cost or cost per service will be. Common add-ons such as special conditioners, treatments, styling, or last-minute client requests may not be included in the basic or initial service price.

Did you know? The adjectives you choose to describe what you want may greatly influence the final outcome. Words like "playful" or "seductive" can evoke some very different images, so being as accurate as possible is important. In some instances it may help to use the word "trendy" instead of "flashy", "tailored" instead of "polished", and "conservative" instead of "classic", but don't stop there. The more you talk, the clearer the picture (and your image) will be in your stylist's mind.

Tips For Duplicating A Haircut You Like

- Write down or remember the words you used when you got what you wanted. Be particularly aware of the adjectives you chose to describe the look you're after.

- During your visit, be as specific as possible. Examples include: "don't cut the bangs"; "cut it up to [*here*] at the sides"; "take off 2" in the back"; and so on. Do this at every appointment--even when being serviced by the same stylist. (Not only because your stylist may not remember the particulars, but because the state of your hair is constantly changing, thereby changing the final outcome.)

- If it's still not quite right towards the end of the appointment time, be sure to tell your stylist so *before* he dries your hair while there's still a little time left. Ask to borrow the comb or run your fingers through your hair when the cut seems about finished, and ask to see the mirror to check basic lengths and shape. (Also see Re-dos in **SALON POLICIES**, p. 64.)

- As soon as you discover that you are pleased with your haircut, note the exact length of the hair in inches at each section of the head. Use examples such as: bangs: 4 inches; length: 1 inch below the shoulders; top layers: 3 inches, etc.

- Since your stylist probably doesn't keep records on haircuts, write down anything that will help *you* to remember what occurred during the appointment which aided in your getting what you wanted as soon as you leave the salon. (Use the **Sample Client Record** in the back of this book.) Pay special attention to certain cutting and drying techniques used on your hair.

Regarding other services: Keep your own records of special products, formulas, procedures, or timing of solutions that are involved in your service whenever possible.

What You Must Always Tell Your Stylist

Before **your service begins, tell your stylist if. . .**

- you have a time constraint.

- you are on medication which could interact adversely with hair and skin products or chemicals.

- you are experiencing any illness which might interfere with your hair, skin care, or therapy. (Massage therapists must know about any discomfort or illness--including a cold or menstrual cycle.)

- there are any products presently on your hair or skin other than cleanser or conditioner.

- you have experienced any scalp, skin, or bodily pain within the past 24 hours.

- your service fee should not exceed a certain amount.

- upkeep of a style, home maintenance, or on-going therapy (where applicable) is an issue.

During **the service, tell your stylist if. . .**

- you experience pain or discomfort during the service being performed.

- you feel wetness or dripping from water or chemicals on another part of your body *not* involved in the service.

- you notice that your clothing or your personal belongings are being damaged or soiled due to the service being provided.

- you know in advance that there is something you will need to do that may interrupt a chemical or delicate procedure.

***After* the service, tell your stylist if. . .**

- you see redness, blisters, or sores on the skin, around nail beds, or on the scalp following service.

- you experience any pain or discomfort within 24 hours following any salon or spa service.

- you notice that clothing was soiled due to chemicals or products used.

Did you know? If your clothing is soiled--say, after hair color--you are entitled to be compensated for your stylist's error or bad luck. Who pays for it? Some salons will cover your loss, but others will take the money owed from the stylist's paycheck. As presumed, independent stylists are on their own.

Just Not Happy?

You have some recourse if you are unsatisfied with your service or service provider (also see The Bad Connection later in this chapter), but it is best to work out any problems with the salon or stylist in question. Check with either the stylist, manager or owner if your options include:

◇ ***A free or discounted re-do from the original stylist.*** First ask your stylist as soon as you know you're unhappy if there is something she can do to fix what is wrong. Most stylists are happy to do a re-do whenever possible, but confirm that the re-do is free or discounted ahead of time to avoid confusion. Also confirm the time frame in which the re-do will be performed.

◇ ***A free re-do from another stylist in the same salon.*** If you and your original stylist don't see eye to eye, or you're simply not comfortable with her work in general but enjoy visiting that salon, find out from the manager or owner if they will allow another staff member to handle your re-do free of charge. (Also see Re-dos in **SALON POLICIES**, p. 64.) Either the owner will pay for it or will take the commission from your original stylist, but it probably won't include the second stylist's tip. If the original stylist is an independent contractor, you'll probably have to pay for someone else yourself.

◇ *Free products, gifts, or substitute salon services*. Maybe nothing can be done about your perm turning out a bit fuzzy, and you're still obligated and willing to pay for all the time and effort provided by the technician, but if you are dissatisfied with your service, don't be shy, and ask for a little compensation. A gift certificate, free bottle of conditioner, or free manicure might be just the thing to ease your disappointment.

◇ *Your money back*. This is a salon's least favorite way of handling your complaint, but most will consider it if your complaint is valid and you refuse other options.

Hint: Whenever possible, pay attention to what is being done throughout the service. If, for example, you were to notice that your nail technician wasn't filing off as much nail as you'd hoped, say something as soon as possible. (After the polish has been applied is not the time to ask for more filing.) Likewise, if your hair is looking redder *during* the coloring process than you imagined, ask why to be sure. Your colorist will either assure you it's just the color of the mix, or will--with further communication--rinse it off and mix up something else if necessary.

The Bad Connection

Whether it was the service, the outcome, or the relationship that went bad, it doesn't matter; you're mad and upset, and you need retribution or compensation before you're satisfied. If the charges you make are serious but not so severe that you are willing to work with the salon for compensation for your inconvenience or distress, see the section titled Just Not Happy (above.) If, on the other hand, you have been injured or angered in such a way that further dealings with your stylist or salon are not an option, **seeking an experienced and reputable professional in another salon is suggested**. Otherwise, there are very few avenues open to the wronged client. Not usually a "hot" enough story for the newspapers and a difficult lawsuit to win--there is little recourse against the licensed stylist, therapist, or technician. Complaints and investigation requests may be made to the state licensing department or Better Business Bureau, but whether you want your money back or a correction for unsatisfactory service, try appealing to your stylist's sense of fairness and integrity before deciding to go to a new stylist or salon.

37

Remember: An independent contractor is just that--independent. The owner of the salon which leases stations to stylists or therapists merely rents the space and does not have to assume liability for his staffs' work in most cases.

Your Stylist's Suggestions:

3

AFTER THE SERVICE--
BEFORE YOU LEAVE

Whether it is obvious that you're finished being worked on or you need to be told that your time is up, either way you'll be happy or. . .not. Did you get what you asked for? Were there any surprises? Are you satisfied with your service? Upon completion, take it for granted that your stylist, technician, or therapist truly wants and expects you to be happy. The salon business is one of the few businesses where **feeling good is always the goal**. But since your stylist may have another client waiting, this may be your last chance to speak your mind, make a last minute change (if there is time), or ask questions. So, at the close of your appointment time, **a)** confirm instructions for home care (if any), **b)** confirm service fees if there is a question, and **c)** if dissatisfied, say so. If you are happy with the results, this is also the time to tell your stylist so, and make a mental or written note of what just transpired. Remember: You want what you want and have planned to pay for it. If you discover at the end of your service that you didn't get what you asked for (or thought you asked for), take the time to mention it before you leave. (See both Just Not Happy in **COMMUNICATING WITH YOUR STYLIST**, p. 36 and Re-dos in **SALON POLICIES**, p. 64.)

Lots-O-Product

At some point in the relationship with your stylist, he will probably recommend a particular product or products. It is okay to question why, but, contrary to what some clients believe, stylists are not in the retail game for big bucks. The truth is, commissions and revenues from shampoos, conditioners, styling products, skin care, and make-up, are hardly worth spending the time to convince a client that she needs them if there wasn't another reason. The fact is, **the better your hair and skin *really* are, the better your hair and skin perform with products!** (And that goes for your nails, too!) There are some who will argue that the expensive professional products sold in salons are no better than the over-the-counter brands sold in the stores. Since the experts on both sides of the issue disagree, the points below can help you decide for yourself if professional products are right for you.

◇ **Concentrated strength**. Products that can only be obtained by professionals--whether from a salon or physician's office--contain the concentrated ingredients which require that purchase of those items be sold with instruction for their intended use. Retail products tend to be watered down for mass, general use--ultimately leaving the product lacking. Best of all, using less product means saving more!

◇ **Protein**. Professional products frequently add the same type of protein to their products as are found in the skin and hair. (Keratin for hair care, collagen for skin.) Commercial products will use various alternative proteins--if at all--which cannot replace the protein you're missing.

◇ **A complete system**. Professional hair care, skin care, and nail care lines formulate their products to work together. With hair care products, for example, the shampoo mildly cleanses the hair, the moisturizer helps the hair retain water, the protein conditioner adds protein to the hair, and the styling products have varying "holdablility"--all containing suitable ingredients at correct pH levels for balance. F.Y.I: Be wary of commercial all-in-one products which may coat the hair and skin with polymers--temporarily adding a layer of synthetic shine to otherwise harsh cleansers.

◇ **Client-requested extras**. What goes into the expense of a professional product is usually what the consumer is asking for, and ultimately, what is needed. These product extras may include: water-soluble ingredients, matching proteins and amino acids, environmentally-sound packaging, a pleasing variety of aromas, botanicals, natural oils, or products that don't use animal by-products or test on animals.

Most importantly, professional products **a)** actually help the hair and skin retain shine and moisture, **b)** correctly prepare the hair and skin before chemical processing, **c)** stabilize the hair and skin afterwards, and **d)** don't coat hair or skin's surface layer with cosmetic build-up. So, the next time you're feeling pressured to buy your stylist's product, you'll know why she wants you to have it: **It's for your own good!** You could spend less money buying cleansers, shampoos, conditioners, moisturizers, and other beautifying treatments in the grocery store, but *less* is what you may be getting in order for the commercial product to keep its cost down.

Did you know? There is a logical explanation if your hair always *feels* and looks better in the salon than at home. See Why It Was Better In The Salon in **HAIR STYLING AT HOME**, p. 76.

Other common questions regarding salon products include:

"What about natural or organic hair and skin care products?"

There is a good reason for the recent trend in natural and organic products: Natural equals health! And botanicals (plant derivatives) are biodegradable and free of potentially earth-sensitive chemicals. Allergy-prone clients are also more attracted to organic products to avoid potentially bothersome artificial substances and fragrances. The bad news? Organic products are not always the best choice for every client. **The lab-developed products have won the hearts of clients who depend on healthier-*looking*, more manageable hair and skin**. In a nut-shell: they tend to work best. In addition, some clients are allergic to natural substances.

"How do I know which products are right for me?"

Most professional lines of hair, skin, and nail care products have several different types of products within their line for various uses or treatment of problems. Professional skin care products, for example, make cleansers for normal, dry, oily and combination skin, humectants to help skin retain moisture, and replenishers to replace the skin's essential oils, amino acids, and proteins. The same manufacturer may also make a complementary line of make-up with various shades and applicators. **Your goal is to find the right combination of products for your individual needs**. But because it can get confusing, it is recommended that you seek the advice of your salon or spa professional--realizing that each is most comfortable with and knowledgeable about the products he

42

uses and sells in his salon. Your choices? You will still have your pick of the many products within the line, and will develop preferences by the way a product works, feels, smells, or costs. (For more on the use of hair products, see Cooking With Hair in **HAIR STYLING AT HOME**, p. 77.)

Did you know? Sometimes mixing different formulations can irritate the skin or scalp, or give a false sense of their effectiveness. Hair, skin, and nail care products are formulated to work together with the products within the same line for a complete and balanced system. Whenever possible, take a "time-out"--1 to 2 days using water or mild cleanser only--to assess how a line is working for you or when switching brands.

PRODUCT ALERT!! Professional products that make their way into retail outlets other than registered beauty supply stores may not be the same product sold by professionals. "Bootlegged" hair and skin care products may look the same on the outside, but do not necessarily contain the same unique formula that makes up the professional brand.

Tips On Tipping

One of the most frequently asked questions is, *"How much should I tip?"* Although 15-20% is the protocol for tipping in restaurants in the US, this percentage is not always appropriate in all salon service situations. Why the confusion? Offering a 15% tip to one stylist for a $50 service would be quite satisfactory to a stylist and most clients, but when the service charge is substantially less or substantially more and involves many salon staffers, this percentage seems unbalanced. Distributing those tips if there are many hands involved can also get confusing. Tally up the total of a whole head of long-haired highlighting, custom or designer permanent, "Day of Beauty", or combination services exceeding $100 with the various staffers, and it's enough to make a client's head spin. Equally as bewildering? Many clients are uncertain how to tip on a $7 -10 eyebrow arch, manicure, beard trim, or nail repair--especially if the stylist or technician has done great work and spent much time with them. Worry no more! Knowing the *average* tip can help any client decide whether to tip more or less.

Average Tips Received Per Service

Shampooers, Coat check, Assistants - $1-$2

Assistants/Apprentices who spend 25% or more time with you - $2-$5

Stylists, Technicians, Therapists providing services between ten and twenty-five dollars - $3-$5

Stylists, Technicians, Therapists providing services between twenty-five and seventy-five dollars - $5-$10

Services seventy-five dollars or more - $7 or more

No-charge re-dos - $3 or more

Note: Tip averages are taken from a sampling of salons in medium-sized cities located in California, Illinois, New York, and Texas, and reflect a combined urban/rural average at the time of publication.

Other common questions regarding salon tipping include:

"Why tip?"

There is no rule that says a client has to tip in a salon any more than a restaurant customer has to tip a wait person. But many clients know that assistants and shampooers work much the way waiters do and make less than minimum wage--really relying on tips. These salon helpers are hired to provide that extra pampering (bringing a beverage, providing a relaxing shampoo, finishing a blow-dry) and help your stylist run on time. Do stylists rely on tips? Some independent stylists refuse tips--having initially set their prices to include their time, skill, and product use. But most stylists work either on a commission basis (which might be as low as 30% of your service charge) or pay rent and additional expenses out-of-pocket to a salon owner--taking home much less than what you pay. Even when a stylist is allowed to set his own prices, since some gratuity is customary, he may keep his prices down leaving the extra "thanks" up to you. Hint: In some cases, good tips inspire stylists to give extra service, discounts, or special products.

"How should I present the tip?"

The reason salon tipping can make a client uncomfortable is because often there is no good place to put it! Restaurant tipping is easy while it's left on the table, and frequent travelers are prepared with small change for tipping taxi drivers and baggage handlers. At your stylist's station, the shelf or counter space might be cluttered or messy, and you don't want to slip it under the sheet of your massage therapist's table since it might end up in the wash! Besides, while you're getting money changed your stylist may disappear into the staff room or begin servicing another client, becoming too enthralled with someone else to be interrupted-- making it more awkward to slip her the money. Just as awkward is fumbling with your money while she's standing there ready to collect! The easiest way to offer a tip? Have the prepared amount that you wish to tip in your pocket in cash and hand it directly to your stylist before walking away. When being serviced in a salon where many people are involved in your care, keep extra singles handy for tipping assistants, helpers, or other technicians. (When tipping several people throughout a salon, you will have to hunt each of them down unless you ask your stylist to distribute those tips.) Better: Ask the receptionist for tip envelopes on which to write *To* and *From* or any other note. And remember, there is no wrong way to tip. Just make sure the tippees know who the tipper is so it can be appreciated!

Did you know? If you leave your tip with the receptionist by including it in your total when paying with a check or charge card at a front desk, it is very likely that your tip will be given to your stylist along with other tips at the end of the day without him ever knowing who it was from.

Maintenance: Until Your Next Appointment

You're about to leave the salon or spa and you look and feel great! *"What would it take to feel like this more often?"* you ask yourself. Well, if your service provider hasn't told you during your service, the time to ask about at-home care and maintenance is right before you walk out the door.

☑ *Products*. Unless you're stylist handles your bill and product transactions directly, what you need and whether or not you need it should be discussed with your stylist before you pay your bill at the front desk. Keep in mind that the receptionist is also usually knowledgeable about the products sold and recommended by your stylist. Some salons only carry one line of products while some carry a wide array of different products. And included within one "line" of hair or skin care products is an array of products for a complete and balanced system. Oils, lotions, soaps, candles, brushes, and various implements and decorations for hair, skin, and nails are just a few of the items that may also be found behind the counter. (For more on products see Lots-O-Product in the beginning of this chapter.)

☑ *Return appointments*. There is nothing more frustrating than the moment you realize you need another appointment for that fresh feeling or special occasion, only to discover that you can't get an appointment for several days or even weeks! Remember that many salons can make your next appointment as far as 3 months in advance, guaranteeing a day and time. If you're uncertain how often your stylist, technician, or therapist suggests that you visit again for optimal maintenance, be sure to ask.

☑ *At-home instructions*. Your massage therapist suggests that you not to lift heavy boxes for a while and advises you return for deep tissue work on that painful shoulder within another week or two. Your colorist reminds you that your swimming will speed up the fading of your new, glamorous auburn highlights. Your aesthetician recommends a moisturizer with sun screen to protect your skin while on your cruise. And your nail technician lectures you on the reasons you shouldn't peel your nails or scrub pots without gloves. So, with such good, professional advice, why is it so hard to follow? **The fact is, looking and feeling good sometimes requires discipline**. Your stylist or technician can only make suggestions; she can't follow you home to see if you're using excessive heat on your hair--making the split ends you're complaining about even worse. And perhaps advice is ignored because salon and spa services are not exactly life or death, and no one will arrest you for physically abusing your own hair and skin! Remember: If it's important to you, you'll make the investment, do the homework, and not mind a bit!

(For more tips on at-home maintenance and retention of hair color and perms, see each individual chapter in **COLORING, PERMING, & OTHER TREATMENTS AT HOME**, beginning on p. 80.)

Payment

When visiting a salon or spa for the first time, you might encounter any number of ways to pay for your service. Where, how, and who to pay differs from one salon to another, and since it can feel awkward, ask your stylist if it's not clear. If your stylist does not walk you to the front desk, ask if your bill is waiting there for you. (Stylists sometimes inform the receptionist of your charge without you noticing.) And since miscommunication between stylists and reception staff happens occasionally, clarify any fees with your stylist if there appears to be a mistake. If your stylist is an independent contractor, you might pay her right there in her room or at her station when your service is complete. Best advice? Find out what the charge for your service usually is and what payment is accepted when making your appointment. Keep in mind also, that independent contractors may not be able to take any credit cards nor have a lot of cash with which to make change. F.Y.I: Pay special attention to extra charges and ask to see a breakdown of your bill if necessary. Also be aware of cancellation policies to avoid any charges acquired from a previously scheduled appointment. (See Cancellation Policies in **SALON POLICIES**, p. 61.)

Keeping A Record

Your stylist should not be expected to remember everything about the service he is providing you or what your future goals are, just as you are not expected to know all the technical details that pertain to your service. Therefore, you can ask your stylist or technician to keep a file or record on you if you're not sure that he already keeps one--especially concerning chemical processes. Having the *stylist* detail your procedure and formula information will come in handy whether you wish to duplicate the formula next time or not. What about keeping your own records? You can ask your stylist for your formula or other service records, but since the information can be misused or taken out of context, some stylists prefer that all records remain private--even from the client. Other stylists will gladly give you your formula or technique description should you need it when traveling out of town. Tip: In addition to using the **Sample Client Record** in the back of the handbook for any at-home procedures that you apply yourself, it is in your best interest to record any and all information regarding your salon experiences whenever possible.

Gift Ideas

One reason to discover what's out there is to have access to the latest ideas in beautification, preservation, and wellness. Need another reason? Gift certificates. A manicure or pedicure, scalp treatment, aromatherapy candle, scented bath oils, basket of professional brushes, or 30 minute massage-- to name just a few of the services and products available--is hardly ever unappreciated! And even if the salon you patronize doesn't provide some of the services mentioned in this guide, most stylists are at least familiar with what is available and are happy to offer their opinions, make suggestions, and refer outside of their salons. Gift items may also include make-up and jewelry. The biggest sellers? "Day Of Beauty" packages of spa or salon pampering services such as make-overs or customizing your own combination of facials, manicures, hair styling, and skin care services. Many 1/2 day or full day packages also include a healthy meal. Some salons will even take your credit card number, schedule appointments, and tally up the accumulated charges after the chosen services have been rendered to the gift recipient. Important: When paying for salon gift certificates in advance, keep an itemized receipt of payment in case the actual certificate is lost and the salon does not have a record. For more on the services available for gift ideas, see What's New-Extra! Extra! in **SERVICE OPTIONS**, p. 2.

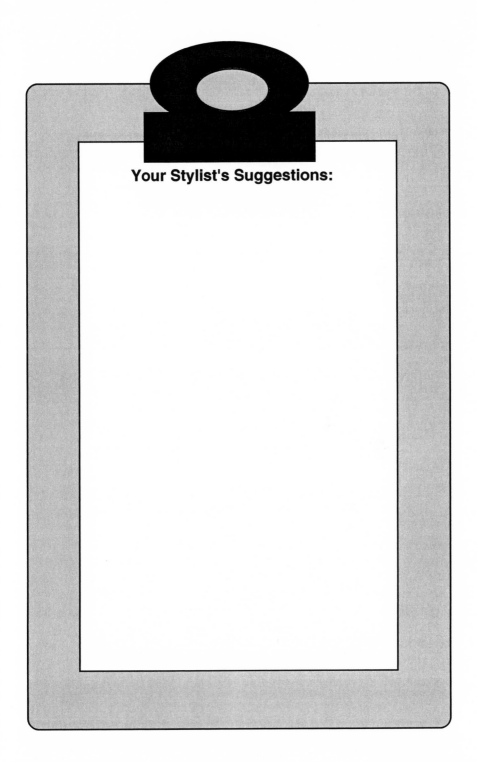

Your Stylist's Suggestions:

4
SALONS

Imagine. . .A quiet salon decorated with a few modern art pieces amongst the simple but elegant stations; a trendy decor with alternative music piped loudly throughout an exciting maze of colorful rooms; an intimate space laced with antiques and cascading flowers with classical music playing in the background; a fun, bustling joint where TVs display several sporting events at once; a relaxed, homey spot with comfy chairs where local conversation is the main attraction. These are just some of the many kinds of salons and spas which can be found, but the ambiance is not always why clients choose a particular place. People usually just 'happen' upon an environment because the salon was either convenient or recommended. However, more often than not, *the environment is a mirror of the staff present*, and when you examine the sheer number of stylists and therapists in salons in any given town you might be glad to know what your options are in the first place! You may even see waterfalls or aquariums in salon waiting areas for that getaway feeling. Other salons provide more of an "other-worldly" experience using the latest in high-tech equipment. Some salons offer a fancy cocktail; others, an herbal drink, while others serve up a great cup of coffee in a paper cup.

You may love the ambiance but not your service provider or the outcome of that service. Or, you may love your server and service, but care less for the ambiance! So keep in mind that there are often as many salons as there are restaurants in any given town or neighboring city. **You *can* find exactly what you're looking for**. And, if you care more about the experience than the relationship with a stylist, find the place first and *then* the stylist--whenever possible--before you fall in love with a magical stylist in a salon you're less than enchanted with. Tip: Phone the establishment first and ask the receptionist to describe what sort of place it is, and if there is a philosophy behind the services they provide.

Did you know? A salon that gives the impression it is "earthy" in name and decor, probably is! Here you'll most likely find natural products and non-invasive procedures. This is just one example of where ambiance and manner of service go hand-in-hand.

The New Spa

Generally, today's spas can include more than full body massages, hot tubs, tanning beds, and steam rooms. Yesterday's innovative cellophane and mud wraps have taken a back seat to today's customized prescriptions for healthy bodies and minds. Today, many spas focus on body detoxification and stress management. Detox can be as simple as applying products to the skin that draw out impurities, drinking healthful concoctions, or incorporating personal nutrition at home for a comprehensive program. Other new ideas include steam tubes which pump stress-reducing aromas and create a "paradise"-like environment, intentionally stimulating every one of your senses. (See What's New--Extra! Extra! in **SERVICE OPTIONS**, p. 2 for more details.) In general, spas may offer skin, nail, and aesthetic services but rarely offer hair services. The main focus of the spa is connecting mind, spirit, and body, for a total relaxing and healing experience. Some also offer meals, chilled lemon water, or herbal health drinks.

Did you know? Even salons are creating a spa-like environment in their shampoo or private manicure rooms with soft music or nature sounds, dim lighting, and lounge-back shampoo chairs with foot rests. Today's working clients demand a more enriching experience--even while taking care of personal business. For this reason, therapies of ancient times such as aromatherapy (stimulating or relaxing the body through the olfactory sense with aromas) or reflexology (stimulating or relaxing the body's organs using massage on coinciding median points on the hands or feet) are making a comeback.

Spas Combining With Medical Groups

Even newer is the trend of spas combining with medical groups and hospitals. Once simply a sanctuary for the soul where the environment was relaxing and pleasing to the senses, now the spa concept of overall wellness may include physicals, vein treatment, sleep-disorder therapy, addiction therapy, acupuncture, neuromuscular therapy, to name just a few. In many cases, skin care specialists and doctors will work together to treat dehydrated, sun damaged or over stressed skin, or with pre- and post-operative stages of cosmetic surgery.

ALERT! Some therapies are performed by aestheticians or certified practitioners trained in their field of study; however, **it is imperative that the service provider's credentials be checked before having permanent, cosmetic, or pharmaceutical-based services administered**. Physicians may also need to be consulted for some therapies relating to wellness.

Wellness Retreats

These days, taking life-enrichment courses are part of a growing trend at wellness retreats. Usually secluded in some fabulous environmental haven, weekend or week-long workshops are available for a fee. Some include every possible permutation of yoga and meditation, relationship courses, awakening sexuality, healing the self, tapping your inner creativity, focusing on Native American or female spirituality, and "happiness" workshops. These programs--in addition to the standard spa concept of exercise, skin care treatments and massage, healthy or vegetarian meals, and room and board--are certain to soothe the mind as well as the body.

Retreats and holistic centers for people with serious illnesses, such as cancer, are also popping up all over the U.S. Special diets, appropriate exercise, and special courses complete the spa's already luxurious setting. It's a double dose of wellness that can have long-term positive effects.

Full service

Specialty

Departmentalized

Convenience

Corporate

Chain

Franchized

Independent Contractor

Types Of Salons

The way in which a salon is run and how your stylist operates may indeed affect your experience in the salon, the outcome of your service, and your relationship with a stylist. Unless you ask, you may not know whether or not a salon is run by a corporation or an individual, or whether each stylist owns his own "station"--each setting up his own little business within a business. **Why would it matter to you?**

There are some common practices typically associated with the different *types* of salons. These differences may include how you'll schedule your appointment, how you'll be treated, to whom you'll give your money, and whether or not you'll get your money back if you're dissatisfied.

If you're the kind of client who likes everything in one place, a **full-service** salon is right for you. Full-service suggests many types of services under one roof--such as hair care, skin care, make-up, nail care, and sometimes massage. Unique services vary from place to place (see **SERVICE OPTIONS**, beginning on p. 1), but you can expect most full-service salons' ambiance to be upscale, modern, or trendy. Most full-service salons offer packages for a "Day Of Beauty" which may even include healthy beverages or meals. And even if you don't wish to visit a full-service salon for yourself, it may be just what is needed for your daughter's wedding party or that special pampering service you owe to yourself. The stylists who work in large full-service operations are usually employees who work under a manager or owner.

53

If you're the kind of client who likes a focused expert, a *departmentalized* salon is the right salon for you. More commonly found in larger cities, the staff hired in these salons are specialists in their particular fields and only concentrate on one type of service. For example, in a departmentalized salon, hair stylists only do hair, nail technicians only do nails, and chemical specialists only do hair coloring and permanents. Although specialists, they will work with other stylists as a team, scheduling your appointments consecutively for a complete look. *Specialty* salons are salons where all the services focus on one area of the business. Examples include nail salons where the entire staff only does nails, skin care salons which only focus on services relating to the skin, spas which only provide pampering services or massage, or hair salons that either only cater to one sex (such as a man's salon with a sports theme), or particular age group (salons for children only.)

If you're the kind of client who likes a fast, no-frills service, a *convenience salon* is the salon for you. These are the fast food of salons. Same name, same ambiance, same walk-in policy for a quick, inexpensive service--generally basic haircuts. You might even see several operations in one city. The best part? Little or no waiting. The disadvantage? Since no appointments are necessary here, your favorite stylist may be unavailable when you arrive--forcing you to see another stylist. Note: Some convenience salons fall under the corporate and franchised heading below.

If you're the kind of client who likes the security of big business backing your service--where executives may make salon policy decisions--**corporate or chain** salons are right for you. These salons may be large or small, full-service or specialty salons, but the same services and products are always available in each. They have firm policies, but ' convenient hours of operation. Here, salon fees only increase systematically. As with any corporate scenario, the manager is your liaison to both the owners and the staff. **Franchised salons** may be as intimate and unique as the staff who make up this salon, but owners still comply with the salon's headquarters' structure. Stylists in these salons may not be able to be as flexible as independent contractors regarding prices and policies, but typically have company support when it comes to continuing education and enrichment programs for their staff. F.Y.I: Employee benefits like vacation pay, insurance, and even stock ownership, create an environment for a stylist to feel secure and "loyal", and less likely to switch to another salon.

If you're the kind of client who truly likes an intimate, one-on-one relationship with an "all-around" stylist, see an **independent contractor**. You can't always tell if stylists are independent contractors, but if each stylist's station area *looks* very different from others in the salon, that's one clue. Recognized for her customized service or personalized working area within the establishment, she is a stylist, technician, or therapist who leases her station, room, cubicle, or area of a salon. This stylist makes her own policies, prices, and hours of operation. Often she orders her own products to use and sell. In this salon, there might be an owner or landlord present, but the stylist is her own boss. Even though there is always the chance that complaints might fall on deaf ears without company support, the independent contractor tends to be the most flexible stylist since she runs her own business.

The Right Salon For You

Whether you are looking to have 1/4 inch of hair trimmed off your one-length blunt hairstyle, a completely new or radical "do", a massage to ease that aching shoulder, or a file & polish manicure, other important things to consider might be: **1)** a particular environment, **2)** special services, **3)** a certain type of service provider, or **4)** your idea of comfortable prices. Prices, ambiance, and a stylist's working style vary from salon to salon. As a client, your preferences will depend not only on the service you desire, but on the entire experience you have in the salon. In a nutshell, you can determine if the environment will be suitable for you by taking some mental notes.

◇ *Walk in and look around*. Much can be deciphered by simply feeling out a salon. How does the receptionist look? Is the environment too loud? Too quiet? Is the mood friendly? Sterile? Sophisticated? Homey? Do the other clients look comfortable? You need to *feel* right about the place where you might develop a relationship with a stylist and return for maintenance--regardless if it's the most popular place in town or not.
Remember: Many excellent stylists have been known to work in less-than-sophisticated-looking salons!

◇ *Know your resources*. When seeking a specific artist's touch, see Finding The Right Stylist For You in **STYLISTS**, p. 67. But when seeking out a particular environment, special service, or specific product, if you've ever said to yourself, "*I wouldn't even know where to find . . .*", contact any of the following establishments to find exactly what you're looking for.

- hotel concierge/chamber of commerce
- fashion/style department of newspapers or magazines
- local beauty supply distributors
- local beauty schools
- local cosmetology association

◇ *Check the Yellow Pages*. Let your fingers do the walking and phone first. This is an especially good way to find a salon if you're new in town or just want to try something new. Call a place that appeals to you and ask questions that pertain to your needs. Regarding hair care, some examples include: "Does the haircut price include the blow-dry (set, curling iron, or style)?" "Is conditioning included in the price of a haircut?" "Are there other extras with that service?" "Is a haircut included in the price of a permanent or hair coloring?" "Are your stylists specialists in one area or does each stylist do everything?"

Your next step might be to visit that salon for a FREE consultation.

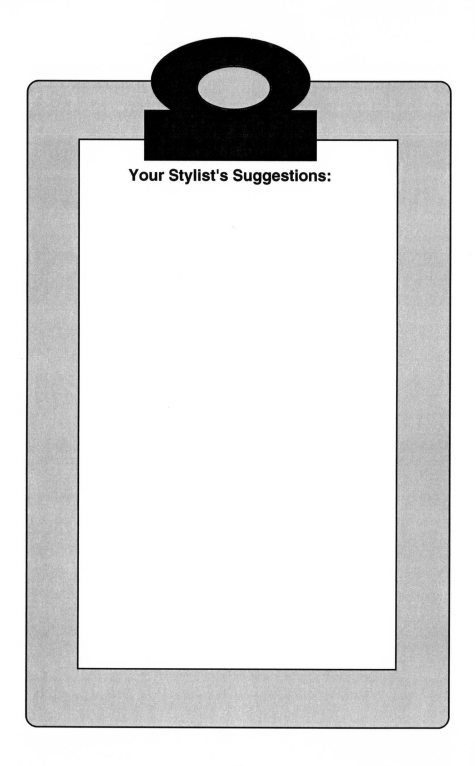

Your Stylist's Suggestions:

5

SALON POLICIES

Ahhh. . .To finally be able to relax and call a new salon "home". No more trial and error. No more need to panic around appointment time! Just schedule and go, right? Perhaps. But make sure you're getting the most out of your salon by finding out which of the basic salon operations and policies below may apply.

Stylist Hierarchy

When each stylist's service price is different even when providing the same service in the same salon, it is usually for one of two reasons: either a stylist's experience allows him to charge more, or the length of time a stylist has worked in that particular salon allows him to charge a higher fee. With titles like "senior designer" or "master stylist", it is difficult to know how and why titles are distributed when one stylist charges $30 for a trim and another charges $60. And sometimes a stylist with many years of experience in a previous salon must start off at the lowest price just because he's the new kid on the block. So, **why see the most expensive stylist?** You may simply want the most senior service provider who has "earned his wings" in his field. In some cases, the higher priced stylists are worth their salt when it comes to challenging or specialized work. Another good time to choose this stylist is when doing something drastically different, new, or controversial. **Why see the least expensive stylist?** The stylist who charges less might still be the most talented and best service provider around. Also, a stylist just starting out may be more enthusiastic, available, and willing to please. This stylist is for the easy-to-please client, clients who need basic, standard services, and clients who find saving money appealing! Curious to find out who's who? Ask the receptionist to explain the salon's pricing structure.

Bang Trims & Other Quick Fixes

Different salons and even individual stylists within those salons may have different policies for quick fixes and touch-ups in-between appointments. Bang trims, nail repair, polish only appointments, spot massages, make-up tips, and eyebrow clean-ups are just some of many. Regarding bang (or "fringe") trims, for example, if the stylist leases a station (an independent contractor who pays the owner rent and makes her own prices and policies), she will either charge a few dollars for the quick appointment (average is $5) or she might offer bang trims FREE to a regular client. Most stylists will only offer one bang trim in-between appointments--which is customary--although some are willing to do quick touch-ups for optimal maintenance as often as needed (as long as it's only a quickie, of course!) To find out your stylist's or salon's policy, always **a)** check first if there is a fee, **b)** see if an appointment is necessary, and **c)** find out whether or not a touch-up in-between is beneficial to your needs or desired goal. <u>Note</u>: Many stylists would rather do your quickie touch-up for free than have you do it yourself at home!

Scheduling

When it comes to scheduling, how much a stylist works and how his services are spaced throughout the day, varies from salon to salon and person to person. How a stylist, technician, or therapist personally schedules appointments depends on one of three things: the salon or spa hours, the arrangement worked out with the manager or owner, or whether or not he is self-employed (independent contractor.) The good news? Although many salons are still closed on Sundays and Mondays, more and more establishments and independent stylists are keeping their salons open all weekend and late into the evening for busy clients. So, whether you prefer an appointment early in the morning, late in the evening, on weekends, or even in the middle of the night, you can probably find a stylist to accommodate your needs. <u>Hint</u>: If your favorite stylist is booked up when you need him, find out if you can get on a "wait list" in case another client cancels--allowing you to fill the appointment time. On the other hand, your stylist might be able to refer you to one of his colleagues in the salon if you can't wait, so be sure to ask your stylist when the receptionist has bad news regarding your stylist's schedule. (See **Return appointments** in the chapter titled **AFTER THE SERVICE-- BEFORE YOU LEAVE** on p. 46 for more scheduling tips.)

Confirmations & "Standing" Appointments

Regarding confirmations: Phoning first can save a lot of time and trouble for everyone while heading off mistakes sometimes made by hard working receptionists and stylists. Besides, your stylist may even be out ill that day, and if you'd rather not be serviced by anyone else, you'll want to reschedule your appointment and save yourself the trip. And if you decide to squeeze in a bikini wax or have your stylist (rather than her assistant) blow-dry your hair, it's okay to call ahead to make sure your stylist will have time to do everything you want to do during your scheduled appointment time. It's even okay to call to ask if your stylist, technician, therapist, or manicurist is running on schedule.

Regarding "standing" appointments: If a "standing" appointment sounds appealing to you (a regular appointment on a certain day and time every week or month), salons and spas are usually able to book your appointments many months in advance. This is particularly helpful around holiday or vacation times. It's also nice to have first pick of the day and time you would like if you know in advance that your service needs are regular; e.g., a haircut every six weeks, a manicure once a week, a massage on Fridays after work, and so on. You might even ask the salon or spa to *call you* to confirm your appointments as a reminder. Remember: Make sure the original appointment is canceled when making changes.

Did you know? The best way to anger a stylist is to simply not show up for an appointment. For most, their time *is* money. Since some stylists are not paid a salary, they lose money if you "no show". Even if you have to call at the last minute, they will appreciate the opportunity to run an errand, eat lunch, or do someone else instead of waiting for you.

Cancellation Policies

Many salons now require a 24 hour notice to cancel an appointment or a small fee is added to your next bill. Some will go as far as to acquire your credit card number for appointments scheduled in advance--especially when the service to be rendered takes several hours. There is no substitute for courtesy on the part of either the client or stylist regarding cancellation notification, but be sure to find out ahead of time what your salon's policies are to avoid a charge.

Becoming A Salon Model

Not all, but many salons need hair, face (make-up), or hand (nails) models. The two purposes in which models might be needed by a salon are for fashion and education. If a salon is active in shows, soirees or photo shoots, stylists tend to look at their clients and their client's friends first for possible models. Some of the pictures you see on the walls of salons and in magazines are not professional models, but everyday clients with no prior modeling experience. Normally, the modeled service is free to the model for giving a salon her time and appendage (hair or nails, etc.) However, each time you agree to be a model, you may be at the mercy of a stylist's artistic ideas which may not otherwise have been something you would have asked for! It may well be a conventional, temporary look you're modeling; but it may also be trendy, outrageous, and permanent. Tip: Always find out ahead of time what the final result will look like and whether you can easily return to your original look if you don't like it.

Even if you're not interested in being a fashion model, you can still "model" for a salon. Stylists that provide in-salon training for the staff or continuing education for assistants are always looking for every type of client to be a salon model. Just as beauty school and massage school students use real people to practice on after working on mannequins and one another, so do stylists in salons, who continue to train even after they've been working in the field and are already licensed. For example, hair salons with assistant/apprentice programs need every hair type on which to practice cutting, styling, and chemical services. And, **if it's not FREE, it's usually very inexpensive**. The result? An excellent service performed by assistants but supervised by senior stylists. The disadvantages? As a model you may have to stay in the salon a bit longer than usual. Appointment times will also be less flexible as you'll have to be at the salon at a given day or night and time when the class is being held.

Children's Services

Although some little people start early getting manicures, massages, basic skin care services, or perms, haircuts are the most common salon service that children require. **The best advice for parents and their young children can be summed up in one idea: kids' salons**. Just as "kid-friendly" restaurants cater specifically to the young customer from the menu to the prices to the decor and crayons, salon owners and stylists are coming up with some innovative ideas for kids. Play areas with toys and books and hydraulic chairs shaped like zoo animals with TV screens planted at eye level for viewing a video tape are just some of the things you might see in a children's salon. Who knows, your child might even keep his head still!

These salons are also a great distraction for the child who is traumatized by the hair cutting process. Certainly, your stylist may agree to do your child's hair and even offer a substantial discount, but observe your adult salon through the eyes of your child and assess whether or not he will **a)** feel comfortable, **b)** make a scene, and therefore **c)** make the hair cutting experience more stressful for both of you. Not only are kids' salons fun and friendly, but the staff is probably more experienced with young clients and the prices are right. Not sure how to find a kids' salon? Their ads are clear in the yellow pages. Also see *Know your resources* in the chapter on **SALONS**, p. 56. F.Y.I: More and more adult salons and spas are now catering to the pre-adolescent client since it's a time when personal hygiene habits are formed. Young girls love to get their nails polished, and it's never too early for a boy to watch dad partake in a professional shave, no-polish manicure, or healthy skin pampering session. (And it makes a great gift for dad, too!) But beware! Many services-- particularly those involving chemicals--will not be offered to children under 16 years of age since young hair is still changing. In fact, sometimes perms and hair color don't even "*take*" on young clients.

Did you know? Many hair and skin care products marketed especially for children are formulated for their specific needs. Their delicate skin, scalp and hair may take a beating with your average adult formulas.

Discounts & Sales

Discounts, if offered, are offered by either the salon or by the individual stylist, and **it never hurts to ask because discounts aren't always advertised**. Some discounts offered by corporations and larger salons include standard discounts to children, students, seniors, government employees, or other corporate affiliates such as mall employees (if the salon is located in a mall), airline employees, travel agencies, or hotel employees and hotel guests. Smaller salons and independent stylists and therapists may offer you a discount if you refer them to your family and friends. If you're lucky, you may even find an individual offering discounted or free services in order to build a new clientele--even if that individual has been doing hair for years but is "new" to an area. Also keep in mind that some individual stylists will alter a service to fit your budget if you're short on cash. Some examples of these altered "short" services to get by on may include customized massage, placing a few highlights in the parting or hairline area only, a quick "file & polish" manicure, or "spot" cutting, coloring, or perming. (Also see Bang Trims & Other Quick Fixes in **SALON POLICIES**, p. 59.)

Salon ***sales*** are either a big part of a salon or spa's marketing strategy or not at all. While some salon owners and retailers believe that a fair, consistent price is the right way to run a business, other retail and service-oriented businesses believe that having a sale is one way to generate business and excitement as well as clear out inventory. Certainly, if you patronize a salon that offers sales, it is not inappropriate to ask the salon receptionist or your stylist if a sale is coming up since sales may be annual or seasonal--at specific times every year. F.Y.I: Sales that are not applied to services might be applied to the salon's products, styling tools, gift items, or health-aids.

Re-dos

Re-do policies vary from salon to salon and stylist to stylist; but a no-charge re-do is usually honored if both the client and the stylist agree there is a problem with the original service. To clarify: Touch-ups and re-dos are not the same thing. A touch-up is *paying* to have more of the same service provided some weeks or more after the initial service.

A re-do is a FREE or less expensive adjustment right after the original service. Actually, requests for re-dos should be communicated to the stylist as soon as possible-- and at least within 2 weeks of the original service--so as to avoid having to work around new growth. If too much time goes by, you may not be eligible for a re-do at no charge due to external factors that are likely to alter any adjustments that could have been made to the original service. For example, if a perm is too loose to begin with, re-perming (if that is what the technician decides) must be performed before too much virgin (unpermed) hair grows in so as to not have to contend with two different scenarios--virgin outgrowth and permed ends. This is just one of many examples where a stylist's approach will vary depending on hair or skin's condition, growth or change.

Therefore, if you know you will require a re-do shortly after being serviced, let your stylist know so he can either re-do or reschedule your next appointment--even if you know before you leave the salon. Better? Live with it a few days at home, and then call as soon as you're sure you'd like or need a re-do. Option: Call and ask for an "adjustment." This may be an easy 15 minutes of your stylist's time to make a slight change. Remember: Don't do anything different than you usually do at home just for your re-do visit. Always show up for all your appointments the way you normally look.

(Also see Just Not Happy in **COMMUNICATING WITH YOUR STYLIST**, p. 36 if your stylist informs you that a re-do is not an option.)

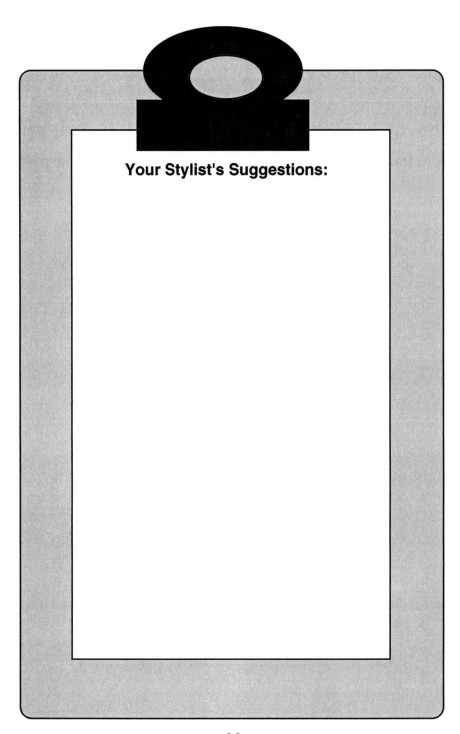

Your Stylist's Suggestions:

6
STYLISTS

The Individual Stylist

Each stylist's work is distinctive due to three reasons: training, experience, and personal artistry. Therefore, it is impossible to get exactly the same service from 2 different stylists--to some clients' dismay. A broader explanation? **Most beauty and wellness professionals combine art with science**. It is equally frustrating when you want consistency but your stylist's approach to *you* differs from one appointment to the next. The reason? If a stylist sees 8 clients a day 5 days a week, and you have an appointment every 6 weeks, he has serviced 240 people before he sees you again. What to do? Make sure any desires, problems, or concerns are expressed during each and every consultation as described in **COMMUNICATING WITH YOUR STYLIST**, beginning on p. 26. Otherwise, a visit to a beauty professional can be terribly stressful--causing clients to hop around endlessly frustrated or to cling desperately to someone whose work they worship--and to feel panic-stricken if their stylist moves. (Also see When Your Stylist Moves in **STYLISTS**, p. 69.)

Did you know? Salon professionals can be flexible about many things as long as it doesn't compromise their artistic integrity. In other words, seldom will a stylist agree to do something he thinks is unattractive, unhealthy, dangerous, or completely lacking a sense of style. Dedicated to his craft, he feels that how you walk out the door carries his signature.

Finding The Right Stylist For You

The best way to find a great stylist or technician? Stop a stranger--whose look you admire--on the street, in a store, on the bus, in a restaurant restroom, or wherever people gather near your home. Better? Scope out people who appear to have similar conditions (hair or skin type), and ask them for the name of their stylist. Most people are quite flattered by this inquiry, so no need to be shy! Again, seek out someone who has at least some of the same qualities as you do-- depending on the service you require. If you have fine, limp, or curly hair, it will do you no good to approach someone whose hair resembles a horse's mane just because you like it. Her stylist might be talented, the salon fabulous; but you won't have any more information than you started out with. Just like finding the doctor, dentist, mechanic, or dry cleaner that you'd trust with your life, finding the right stylist--whether for a one-time service or regular upkeep--can *feel* like finding a diamond in the rough. **A stylist's disposition, interpretation of your needs, and proficiency, will either combine to meet your expectations or not**.

Personalities

Some service providers are flamboyant and talkative; others work diligently and quietly. Unique in personality and performance, there is a stylist for everyone. In fact, what usually attracts a client to an environment or stylist is *like-mindedness* in image or personality. After all, no one cares to spend time and money in a place that feels uncomfortably foreign to them, and no client cares to be serviced by a stylist whose outlook and image is so different that the client's wishes are ignored. This is not to say that a conservative business person doesn't enjoy the artistic, flashy stylist and the experience she might have with that stylist. But in order for the stylist to retain that client or *type* of client, the stylist has to be well-versed in classic, conservative looks that keep in mind the client's personal style, business image, and maintenance objectives. Fortunately, personality mismatches become less important with careful communication regarding the service *before* any work is performed, and if necessary, before a client even agrees to being worked upon.

What The Community Dictates

Just as the flamboyant stylist can provide a conservative service, so can many conservative stylists in a modest, rural salon be trusted to do an updated urban or trendy 'look'. Similarly, small-town massage therapists, manicurists, and aestheticians may also use the latest products and be well-versed in the latest techniques. However, chances are that the stylist working in a rural area will ultimately be more experienced in providing 'looks' and services which cater to the clientele in that area. These clients may not be impressed by the posh environment of a ritzy, urban salon or into the latest trends. Depending on supply and demand, they might also not support services like body healing or "dreadlocks", or any number of unique services which cater to a specific subculture. In other words, **if a small community doesn't require it, it may not be on the salon or spa menu**. Conservative and classic looks, permanent waves, a no-nonsense massage, and great nails may be on *that* menu. In this same salon, men might appreciate uncomplicated cuts and women might find stylists more experienced in "up-dos" for galas and weddings, rather than in a trendy salon with stylists trained to do mainly "wash & wear" precision haircuts. On the other hand, almost any kind of service that exists--as well as a wide range of salon environments--can be found if you're willing to take the city drive *and* pay the price. Usually, but not exclusively, the ultra-pampering and latest products and techniques are found in the salons and spas located in larger towns and cities. (See What's New--Extra! Extra! in **SERVICE OPTIONS**, p. 2, and The Right Salon For You in **SALONS**, p. 55.)

When Your Stylist Moves

Ask most salon owners and they will tell you that their staff is ever-changing. Why? Because salon and spa employees must have a comfortable balance between autonomy and support from the owner. Even independent contractors who lease stations have agreements as to what the owner will supply and how the rent will be increased over time. Some clients believe that the reason stylists move around so much is, because as artists, they must be unstable and temperamental. More accurate would be to say that because there are so many choices open to this type of artist, that she will make the changes necessary to suit her *and* her clientele.

Has your stylist left without warning? Some stylists keep their own records with their clients' names, addresses, and phone numbers, while others are not allowed by the salon to take your information. Salons with integrity will let a stylist's clients know where she has relocated while at the same time offering you an alternative stylist--letting it be your choice as to whether or not to stay with that salon--but whoever answers the salon phone may not know the details of your stylist's relocation. Tip: If you don't want your stylist to lose track of you, make sure she has your current address and home and work phone numbers.

What About Stylists' Training & Licenses?

Do you ever wonder how your stylist's education and licensing requirements affect you? Did he apprentice, assist a master designer, or just get out of beauty school? Does your stylist attend more schooling to renew his license? As with many professions, it's no secret that a license, the proper experience, and professionalism do not necessarily go hand in hand. And in this industry, **beauty schools and apprenticeships are only the beginning of where stylists learn how art and science come together**. Unfortunately for the consumer, there is no "formula" for a successful stylist, technician, or therapist, or for the service provided by one. And because every state has different requirements for each type of license (with some practitioners not even required to have a license), only general educational and licensing requirements are mentioned below.

In general, beauty schools offer a student the opportunity to acquire either an "umbrella" license (training for hair, some skin care and nail services) or separate training for an aesthetician's or manicurist's license only. In addition to the academic curriculum, students provide services to willing clients in the clinic or academy salon under the supervision of a licensed instructor. A mock state board exam is given in school before the state inspector's test is taken for the state license.

One reason you might care? As a consumer you might be interested in being serviced by a trainee at a school clinic to save money. Even while in school or just fresh from graduating, a talented, enthusiastic stylist who loves what he's doing may be the best ticket in town. The risk? Although supervised, many students will still require more skill and speed before being able to satisfy the majority of their clients. F.Y.I: Specialty schools (e.g., various massage, make-up, image, or consulting schools) are separate institutions from the average "beauty" or cosmetology school, and each has its own specially designed curriculum and certification program.

More On Licenses

Since it can be difficult to locate the state department which handles licensing for cosmetologists, massage therapists, and so on, you can call any local beauty school found in the yellow pages to obtain information on *your* state's license and registration requirements.

Cosmetologist/All Around Stylist - In order to legally work on someone's hair, graduation from beauty school and acquisition of a license after passing a state board test is mandatory in all states. The hours of written and practical education in school vary from state to state with some requiring both a practical and written test, and some requiring only a written state board exam. In New York state, for example, 1000 beauty school hours are needed for a cosmetologist's license. 1500 hours of beauty school are required in Texas and Illinois, and 1600 hours in California.

New York and California still require cosmetologists to pass both a written and practical state exam, while Illinois now requires only the written portion. The cosmetologist's training provides an "umbrella" license which allows the service of hair, nails, basic skin care, facials, and sometimes massage. This umbrella does not include men's shaves (which can only be given by barbers) and in some states, full-body massage and certain skin care treatments. Separate, individual licenses for manicuring, aesthetics (skin care), and electrolysis (hair removal), are available.

Barbers - While barbers and cosmetologists train in many of the same areas, including hair cutting, coloring, perming, skin care, and nail care, barber school focuses on men's services with extensive training in men's haircuts and shaves. And because the barber school curriculum touches on all the major salon services--with the exception of hair setting--the hour requirements needed for a barber's license are similar to a cosmetologist's. What *can't* a barber do? Waxing (hair removal) from the shoulders down. The cosmetologist, on the other hand, is not licensed to use a razor on the face. (For more on men's services, see Not Just, But Especially For Men in **SERVICE OPTIONS**, p. 21.)

Nail Technician - Like hair stylists, nail technicians are required to have a state license, but the beauty school requirements (or "hours") are not as long since hair and skin care education is not necessary. In Illinois, only 350 hours are required to perform services for the hand and nails. 250 beauty school hours are required for a manicurist's license in New York, 400 in California, and 600 in Texas. F.Y.I: In recent years, the nail industry heard and answered the call to increase education concerning sanitary measures to guarantee cleaner tools and safer methods for their clients.

Chemical Technician - Anyone with a cosmetologist's or barber's license can become a specialist in chemical application (tinting, perming, and hair relaxing), but should **a)** have extensive experience and education beyond what is taught in beauty school, and **b)** solely provide chemical services for optimal experience and concentration in order to call herself a specialist. Hint: Being proficient with tints, dyes, perms, or straighteners can be a stylist's "specialty", but make certain this title is deserved where delicate or corrective work is needed. How do you check? Ask the salon receptionist to refer you to the most experienced technician in the salon and specify if it is for color, perm, or relaxer. Better? Have free consultations with more than one chemical technician--including a specialist in a departmentalized salon. (See Types Of Salons in **SALONS**, beginning on p. 53.)

Skin Care Specialist/Aesthetician - Technicians who provide services such as facials, hair removal, body wraps, scrubs, brow arching, or lash tweezing and tinting (to name just a few skin-beautifying services), are also required to keep an up-to-date license. 750 beauty school hours must be acquired before being allowed to provide skin care services in a salon or spa in Illinois. California, Texas, and New York require 600 hours of skin care education in beauty school. Aestheticians who use special machinery must have additional training and be certified. (See Skin Care Services in **SERVICE OPTIONS** beginning on p. 15.) Electrologists (beauty professionals who perform electrolysis hair removal) should also have special training and the appropriate license. Remember: Always consult a physician before doing any invasive treatment.

Make-Up Artist - In order for a make-up artist to apply make-up and provide other various services under this title in a salon or spa, she must have a cosmetologist's or aesthetician's license. Make-up artists who are trained by product companies to sell make-up--as in department stores--do not need certification to sell it, but do if they apply the make-up to your face. Important: Every make-up artist must have additional certification when using machinery, applying chemicals, or applying permanent make-up.

Massage Therapist - Cosmetologists and barbers can apply massage techniques above the shoulders, while aestheticians massage the face, neck, and shoulder area. However, anyone giving any type of full body massage must endure intense, specialized training--even in states where a license is not required to perform massage. Massage schools of various disciplines (Swedish massage, Shiatsu massage, etc.) offer courses that include anatomy and require students to practice massage on clinic clients. At the present time, only a handful of states require that massage therapists have a state license. New York does require massage therapists be licensed, but California, Illinois, and Texas do not. The good news? Even in states where a license is not required, there is state *registration*, which involves passing a written and/or practical test given by the health department.

Special Note: With the exception of health care consultants, most salon *fashion and beauty consultants* are not required to have a state license but may have obtained specialized training with a certificate program. (For more, see Consultants in **SERVICE OPTIONS**, p. 3.)

Salon owners, receptionists, and managers, are also not required to be licensed as long as they are not performing hands-on services, but the salon itself must be registered so that sanitary laws, building codes, and general operating practices are followed. In addition, stylists working from their homes must also have salon and independent contractor's licenses.

Did you know? Although required in many states, some beauty professionals do not openly display their licenses as do doctors. The best way for a client to find out about a stylist's or technician's background? Begin by asking what kind of training they had to have to get where they are today.

Continuing Education

Continuing education for license renewal for salon professionals is only mandatory in a few states. This licensing law makes it mandatory that stylists seek further education after beauty school by attending classes or shows in the beauty industry. In states where continuing education is *not* required for license renewal, only a fee for registration and sometimes a medical exam is required every couple of years. With or without the continuing education law, trade shows, conventions, soirees, teach-ins, classes, and competitions are available in every city and town throughout the year making it easy for stylists, technicians, and therapists to stay abreast of the latest styles, find out about new products, and learn specialized techniques. Fortunately, even where continuing education is not mandatory, most stylists insist on attending several shows or classes each year. Find out if your stylist is interested in this type of growth.

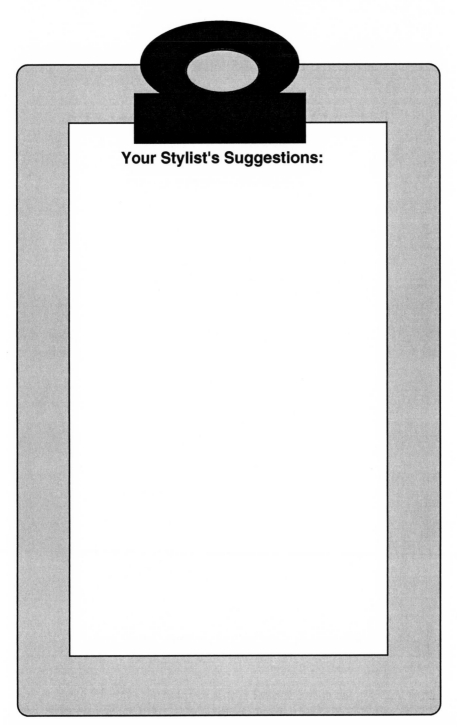

Your Stylist's Suggestions:

7
HAIR STYLING AT HOME

Doing It Your Way

A common complaint of many clients is that they are unable to duplicate a similar salon look after they get home when left to their own devices. To help correct this problem, some salons now offer appointment times for clients to get styling lessons. Keep in mind, however, that some hairdos are not intended to be duplicated at home. Another common complaint? *Not* being happy with the way the hair was finished in the salon, but liking it fine once redone at home. Either way, when it all comes out in the wash, you'll have to work with your hair *your way*. (For styling tips, see Cooking With Hair later in this chapter.) <u>F.Y.I</u>: If after a few days you decide to return to your stylist for a re-do, you'll need to contact your stylist by phone within a few days and schedule another appointment since no-charge re-dos may not be honored after a week or two. (See Re-dos in **SALON POLICIES**, p. 64.)

Why It Was Better In The Salon

Perhaps the cuticle (top layer) of the hair was less *ruffled* by the stylist. At home you might ruffle the cuticle more by rubbing the towel on your hair too much or by being too rough on it--making it look frizzier. Also, the stylist might use certain products in a way that creates a look difficult to duplicate at home unless the products are applied in the same amount and in exactly the same manner. Another explanation? Perhaps the stylist can more easily dry the hair in smaller sections standing above you. Your hair also begins to dry while it is combed smooth during the cut or service--resulting in a smoother look. In other words, it is just the stylist's technique. But don't give up. Talk to your stylist to see if you can learn it, too! <u>Tip</u>: Some stylists offer styling lessons so a client can practice using a blow dryer with specific brushes and products, learn to "scrunch" permed hair, or learn any number of other styling techniques.

Why It *Wasn't* Better In The Salon

Some clients complain that their stylist spends too much time primping and fussing over their hair when they're just going to run home to rewash and style it themselves. If you like your hair better at home than in the salon, it's probably because only you know just how you like to wear it! What to do? First try determine whether or not the basic service (haircut, perm, or color) is to your liking. If it's just the *finishing* that you don't like, try to instruct your stylist how you'd like your hair styled before he begins. If you'd still prefer to do it yourself, ask your stylist if you can do it yourself right there in the salon. Some stylists are willing to hand over their equipment for you to have at it. However, If you do finish your hair yourself, your stylist will probably still want to check your haircut, hair color, or perm before you leave.

Thinking about cutting your own hair?

Even the most gifted stylists will attempt to cut their own hair and regret it later. With the exception of trimming one's bangs or fringe around the face, it is nearly impossible to do a good, thorough, and accurate job yourself. One reason is dexterity! Most people can't work on the back or sides of their heads with ease. Another reason is perspective. The front may look all right, but the "dot-to-dot" blending game of most haircuts requires skill. Still, some will succeed, and others will cry. If you are determined, however, or certain you'll lose control and grab those shears on a desperate evening, talk to a stylist first for some tips. She'll probably try to talk you out of it, but you might get her to show you a trick or two. (Well, maybe just for the bangs!)

Cooking With Hair

Ever notice how simple food items taste differently just by the way they are prepared? Whether baked, broiled, sautéed, barbecued, or pan fried, different cooking methods bring about very different dishes--not to mention the difference in appearance on the plate. When you add herbs, spices, seasonings, sauces, or other condiments, the combinations of tastes and presentations are simply endless. And so it is with hair. Some have more flexible hair than others, but **hair has the ability to change when different styling/finishing techniques are combined with different products**.

Since it virtually impossible to describe all the different ways this can be accomplished, it is suggested that you discuss this idea with your stylist and practice some ideas at home in your own bathroom. The following are just some tips to get you started.

- If you usually use styling gel, try using another fixative such as a shine polymer, styling lotion, alcohol-free mousse or styling spray. Who knows, your hair just might do something it has never done before!

- If you typically use styling lotion, gel, mousse, or any hair care product *before* drying your hair, try applying your favorite fixative to the hair *after* the hair has been dried instead! (Unless, of course, the manufacturer or your stylist instructs you to only use the product one way.)

- Do you always blow-dry your hair? Only let it air-dry? Do you always brush it back or forward when you dry it? Never use a brush at all? Just as combining a variety of products can change the look, feel, and manageability of your hair, so can the use or lack of heat and other various styling tools *with* those products. <u>Good Advice</u>: Watch your stylist, talk to your stylist, experiment together. <u>Best Advice</u>: Break out of that same old way you do your hair and get creative!

(For more on products, see Lots-O-Product in **AFTER THE SERVICE--BEFORE YOU LEAVE**, p. 40.)

Hair Decorating And Ornaments

Want a wild, crimpy wave? Admiring someone's messy up-do held together with only a colorful rod? Curious about the hair ornament gadget advertised on cable TV? Available for hair decoration are a variety of heated irons and plates as well as various combs, clips, and gadgets to choose from on the store shelves. Whether you need to trick problem hair into submission or want a quick, fashionable style, there are colorful, useful items for decorating short, medium, or long hair. Although available at grocery and department stores, a larger selection can be found at your local beauty supply store. Consult a stylist for tips on ideas and instructions for use. <u>Tip</u>: Beauty supply store employees are also a good source for advice on the "how-to's" of hair decorating.

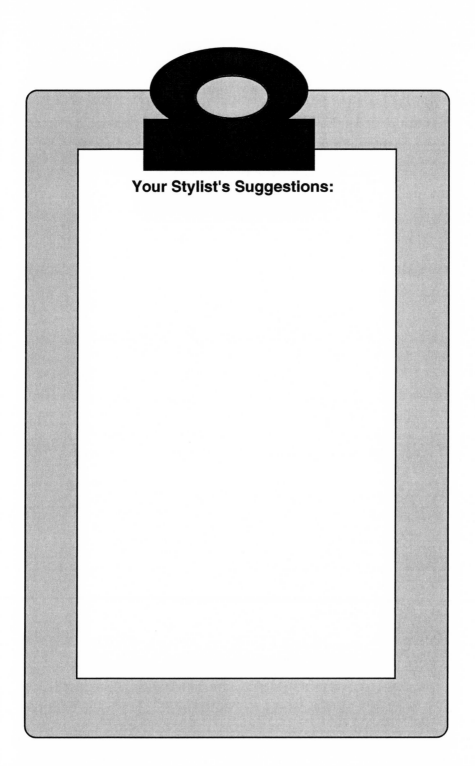

Your Stylist's Suggestions:

8

COLORING, PERMING, & OTHER TREATMENTS AT HOME

The shelves are packed with a variety of do-it-yourself salon kits from coloring, perming, and relaxing hair, to skin treatments and hair removal. And as long as you follow the directions there's no problem, right? **WRONG!** Take heed of the following rules before deciding whether or not to do-it-yourself at home.

5 Rules For Doing Chemicals At Home

☑ *Rule #1.* **NEVER** apply chemicals to hair or skin where sores, redness, blisters, cuts, or irritation of any kind are present.

☑ *Rule #2.* **NEVER** apply a chemical over an existing chemical at home. Normal processing procedures may require a different approach when applying a second substance or solution to the hair or skin. Timing might need to be cut in half for processing, but most importantly, pre- and post-preparation is crucial. One example includes wearing both hair color and a permanent wave. Even if you have successfully applied one to your hair, let a professional apply the other.

☑ *Rule #3.* **NEVER** reapply any solution(s) after the completed processing has taken place to avoid over-processing. (Additionally, once bottles have been opened or mixed solutions have been left out for a long time, they will be weakened or useless.)

☑ *Rule #4.* **ALWAYS** be aware that many procedures <u>cannot</u> be reversed. Some mistakes from chemicals are permanent until hair is cut off, skin heals, or nails grow out. Other chemicals must be applied to camouflage the problem--when possible. Keep in mind that corrective procedures for hair and skin are *not* an exact science. (See Corrections For Color (& Perms) in **SERVICE OPTIONS**, p. 9.)

☑ *Rule #5.* **ALWAYS** use caution with chemicals and follow directions completely. If you let a batch a cookies bake a few minutes too long, they'll just be a little scorched. Leave a strong chemical on your hair or skin a few minutes too long, and the damage may be severe.

Reasons To Do Chemicals In The Salon

- Less chance for over- or under-processing.
- Access to better cleansers, conditioners, developers, processing and neutralizing solutions, hair and skin rejuvenators.
- Access to a variety of *intermixable* colors and solutions.
- Same day hair cutting before or after a chemical service with finishing for completion and balance.
- Information on complementary make-up or wardrobe colors in conjunction with hair color services provided by salon staff.
- Explanations and education regarding care and maintenance provided by salon staff.

Still hooked on doing it yourself? Read on for some general tips!

Hair Coloring At Home

If the hair is in good, virgin condition (no chemicals whatsoever on the hair), as a *general* rule, coloring hair **darker** with store purchased hair color may be successfully achieved. Since color is being *deposited* either into or onto the hair (depending on the type of color chosen), the procedure is often similar to staining a piece of wood or coloring a piece of paper with watercolors. Temporary or semi-permanent hair color only stains the surface of the hair, while more permanent color will enter the hair shaft where the hair's pigment is altered--despite inevitable fading--until that hair is again altered in some way or cut off. Although depositing color is easily attained whether the natural color is light or dark, **once the hair is darkened it is difficult to lighten again easily**. In the worst case, a harsh bleaching process is the only hope for color removal, and as a result, the hair will be much less natural-looking and feeling. So, considering that without the right products and proper technique you may not be at all pleased with the initial result, ponder the following questions before going darker at home.

◇ **How dark?** If you are a "light" brunette who is lacking shine and looking for a richer, lustrous color, a home hair coloring box-kit may be beneficial. The same goes for a light blonde or light redhead looking for the most subtle, *richer* change. When the desired color is several shades darker than the natural color, however, it is important to consult a professional since preparation of the hair may be necessary for achieving an attractive, even color. And remember, only a professional can mix several colors together or vary the strength of the developer to get just the right shade and tones for any hair color. (Also see Going Lighter With Hair Color later in this chapter.)

◇ **How permanent?** With so many categories of hair coloring products available on the grocery store shelves, making the right purchase for your needs can be the trickiest part of doing color at home. Terms like "wash-in color", "vegetable dye", "semi-permanent", and "tone on tone" color can be very misleading to someone who has not done her homework. Regarding permanency, the recommendation for first-timers doing color at home is to **always use the *least permanent* type of hair color whenever possible**. Most manufacturers of hair color will have different categories of color which may include: a cumulative metallic dye promising to darken the hair gradually, a bleach product which strips and lightens color permanently, and tints of various strengths and permanency in-between that lift and/or deposit color. And while going darker or adding vibrant tones are safest for at-home use, using a color that will wash out--if uncertain--is a good way to test the hair's (and your) response before deciding to go more permanent at a later date. The biggest problem? Not getting a complete picture of what a more permanent color will look like since permanent colors have more depth and tone. It will, however, give you some sense for whether or not to continue.

◇ **Saving how much money?** When clients were asked why they did their color at home rather than by a colorist in a salon, the most common reason was cost. But consider this: Technicians who specialize in and only do chemical services get an average of 5 appointments or phone calls per week requesting corrective work or information on re-dos from at-home jobs gone wrong! Many clients who attempt a correction themselves will most likely spend up to *3 times* what it would have cost them to have their color done right the first time. (This is assuming a correction is even possible!)

For information on corrections, see Corrections For Color (& Perms) in **SERVICE OPTIONS**, p. 9.

Going Lighter With Hair Color

While there is some potential for success in using at-home color when *depositing* color, **lifting or stripping the hair at home to achieve a lighter shade is almost never recommended**. In fact, so many problems can result from trying to lighten natural color that colorists often schedule extra appointment time in case the need to make adjustments arises. Here are a few reasons why:

◇ ***One bottle doesn't always do the job***. The client with medium brown hair hoping to be blonde will be sorely disappointed when the box of blonde hair color and developer turns her medium brown hair into light golden or "brassy" brown. The reason? It's simply a matter of chemistry. Even experienced colorists must fight dark hair each step of the way to blonde. It can be accomplished easily and beautifully by experienced professionals with minimal damage to the hair, but factors including the hair's condition, colorability, and present hair color must be taken into consideration. Only then can the hair be taken through a variety of steps of lightening and depositing. Brunettes simply can't get a light blonde in one step at home.

◇ ***There is no such thing as drab hair color***. Since lifting one's natural hair color to a lighter shade brings out a lot of unwanted red and gold tones in the hair's pigment, hair coloring products contain "ash" base colors of green, blue, and violet to help neutralize those tones. Unfortunately, even *ashy* formulas cannot totally eliminate the warm glow. In fact, brunettes who once considered themselves "naturally ash" or "without warmth" will complain of more red or gold tones present throughout the hair after having lightened it--even after using the most ash that one can use to keep it drab. <u>Note</u>: A truer ash color can be achieved on hair that is naturally blonde or pre-lightened with tint or bleach.

◇ ***Color "takes" differently from roots to ends***. This is another reason that professionals employ so many steps. Hair at the root or near the scalp is called a "heat zone." This area--up to approximately 2 inches out from the scalp--is where color processes the fastest and sometimes, the easiest. In other words, you might get the desired color throughout this area of the whole head, while the middle of the hair shaft will be one color, and the ends, another color. <u>Note</u>: There are exceptions to this rule, and in some cases the ends or previously processed hair will either take the color fastest or be more problematic. Additionally, the length of the hair also plays an important factor in how a color "takes." The shorter the hair, the easier it is to lighten evenly and effectively.

◇ ***Blondes don't always have more fun***. The most frustrating thing for a colorist is trying to convince the dark-headed client that blonde may not be right for her. It might be due to her natural skin tone, eyebrow color, or entire color scheme that would clash with light hair color. And as if nature herself fights the process, bleach--instead of the less harsh high-lifting tint--is the only thing that will lift very dark hair enough to put it into a blonde category. The bad news? Bleaching the hair can take many hours, require many processes, and even cause scalp pain before the hair reaches the desired lightness. At best, the hair and scalp will survive the processes, and the hair will take on a somewhat natural look if toned properly.

Did you know? Tint won't lift tint. Do you already have hair color and still want it lighter? Some color removers barely budge the hair color that is present, especially if the shade is dark. The answer? A bleach product or similarly strong lightener. But don't expect a natural-looking hair color when you're through.

Two specific situations where lightening at home is not *as risky* are:

1) Highlighting hair that is naturally blonde, or

2) Permanently lightening (tinting) or stripping (bleaching) hair that is naturally blonde *and* short.

Why? In a nutshell, **there is a shorter distance between light and lighter with fewer variables to contend with**. In other words, whether subtly highlighting or lightening an entire head of hair, the darker the natural hair color or the further the natural shade level is from the desired level, the harder it is to attain the desired result.

Temporary Fashion Colors

Perhaps the only color recommended for safe application at home, temporary color comes in the form of sprays, gels, liquid, shampoos, conditioners, and mousse. Temporary color also comes in natural-looking or fun, fashion colors. It doesn't have to be Halloween to be in the mood for purple streaks to match your new nail polish; and a little auburn hue might be just the thing for your mousy brown hair. Besides, you can wash temporary color out the very next day, right? *Usually*. Keep in mind the following facts:

◇ **Fun vs. Natural**. Always check to see if the temporary color is designed to result in flamboyant, bold color, or designed to add a subtle, translucent, earthy hue. Note also, that the color of the *color* may appear brighter or more intense at first glance than what actually results on the hair--not giving you a clear indication. Not sure? Test the color on a portion of hair that is hidden underneath top layers.

◇ **Permanency**. The lighter your natural hair color, the brighter and more permanent the color could be--despite the fact that a color is "temporary". Although each manufacturer's product is different, very vibrant fashion colors have been known to hang on to blonde hair for weeks.

◇ **Feasibility**. Some colors just don't show up on dark or resistant hair. Blues, blonde shades, and pinks are barely visible on dark hair (if at all), and temporary natural shades tend to just slide off resistant gray hair. Sometimes, a more permanent solution, or chemically preparing the hair prior to using temporary color does the trick.

Which Hair Color Should You Buy?

Ask a colorist what's in the grocery store hair color aisle, and he either hasn't familiarized himself with boxed color, or he won't want to confuse you with the dizzying maze of options. If, however, he's willing to help you choose an at-home hair color for convenient in-betweens, out of town pick-me-ups, or to save an occasional dime, what he can help you with is choosing the right *category* of hair color. How do you choose in the sea of boxes with pretty women sporting various hair color shades on the front? Without having done your homework first, you might stand there for hours, so here are a few tips:

◊ **The price range**. Never choose a hair color because it's cheaper or on sale. Then again, don't be fooled into thinking the most expensive is the best. It is imperative that you know what *category* of color you need first. Then, you may have 2 or 3 brands to choose from--the more expensive hair color having the latest formulas and conditioners. <u>Hint</u>: Once you know exactly what shade you want, look for the same shade in a cheaper brand or with one that uses coupons for your next touch-up. If you don't love it as much, go back to the original formula the following month.

◊ **The swatches**. Some manufacturers have included samples of colored hair swatches next to the boxes of color to help you better visualize what the hair should look like. To get an even better understanding of what the color will look like on you, read all of the descriptions of possible outcomes included in or on the box.

WARNING! Your natural or present hair color affects how a formula will "take" on your hair. When looking at swatches to determine what you want, keep in mind that the original color of the manufacturer's swatch is different than your hair color before it was tinted or stained.

◊ **Names**. Names like "Fire Engine Red" or "Moonglow Brown" should not entice you into choosing a hair color, but may give you some sense of the outcome--even though the images they evoke are subjective. As for other catchy labels, be aware that each manufacturer may carry three or four different categories of color: **temporary** (1-2 shampoos), **semi-permanent** (6-12 shampoos), **demi-permanent** (4-6 weeks), and **permanent color** (fades, but remains)--so careful attention must be paid to the *kind* of color it is as well as the specific shade and tone.

◇ ***Beauty supply vs. Grocery store.*** Usually, you can only purchase "user-friendly" products without a license. In other words, since drastic changes--like going from brunette to blonde--requires many products and possibly complicated procedures, fast-working bleaches and certain hair color are only sold to professionals. Grocery stores have even less of a selection--except for low-risk hair color. <u>F.Y.I</u>: Beauty supply stores sell professional styling aids, cleansers, moisturizers, and "user-friendly" color and perms to non-professionals.

AT-HOME TIPS FOR HAIR COLOR RETENTION:

• Wash the hair as little as possible. (Rinsing and conditioning are okay.)

• Don't swim in chlorinated or salt water.

• Don't expose your hair to excessive heat with dryers, irons, or sunlight.

• Use products that help. Examples include appropriate color enhancing or neutralizing shampoos and conditioners, cleansers and moisturizers for tinted or bleached hair, color sticks or wands to temporarily cover up outgrowth, and styling products sensitive to chemically treated hair.

Perming Or Relaxing At Home

As with hair coloring, curling and straightening hair is best performed in the salon by a person who is experienced with the chemicals to be used. While it is certainly true that many women pass down their knowledge of how to chemically treat their locks from generation to generation--often with better results than some professionals with less experience--**it should never be assumed that an untrained person is more familiar with the chemicals and their reaction than the professional**. If, however, your hair is in good condition (strong, healthy-looking and feeling) and is virgin (no other color or perm chemicals present), you are the only recommended candidate for using a home perm or relaxer. The do-it-yourself perms are fine products that produce fine results when used correctly. Still, keep in mind that only a perm technician can **a)** customize your perm, **b)** prevent overlapping on previously chemically treated hair, **c)** wrap with even tension, and **d)** balance and complete the perm.

The biggest risk? If proper neutralization does not take place, the hair could literally break off. Neutralizing stabilizes the hair and stops the perm or relaxer from being over-processed. If not applied completely, properly, and at just the right moment, this oversight could have devastating consequences. In addition, what doesn't break will probably have to be cut. Other problems can occur, too. *Under*-processing leaves the hair in manageable condition, but usually cancels any idea of getting the desired results until *that* hair is eventually cut off. Still determined? Below are a few questions to ask yourself or discuss with a technician before attempting an at-home perm.

◇ *How curly? How straight?* If a "body wave" is what you're after, you may have better luck with a home perm kit than if you attempt an all-over curly or designer perm that requires a polished technique. With a looser curl, even the straight bits from a less-than-perfect wrap will be less noticeable. You will also have more success with a home relaxer kit if your goal is to relax the hair *slightly* rather than attempting to make it stick-straight. Here, the less time the chemical is left on and manipulated through the hair, the less chance there is for over-processing and subsequent damage. It will also matter less if some areas are straighter than others. What variables determine curl or straightness? Rod size is the main factor in determining curl size, and the technique used for manipulating curl determines straightness--as long as solution type and appropriate timing are taken into consideration. Furthermore, how you contend with all the other variables such as texture, porosity, density, length, present haircut and hair shape, present amount (of lack) of curl, other chemicals or cosmetic weight, will determine your success rate. Even medication taken orally can interfere with chemicals applied to the hair, so it's no wonder with the endless combination of variables that each approach to an individual's perm or relaxer will produce different results--even when the same tools and products are used. In fact, **even the slightest modification of variables from time to time will produce different results** *on the same head of hair*. Confusing? If your perm was better the last time you did it, ask yourself what was different about your hair then. Were you perming over old perm this time? Was your hair longer last time? Shorter? Layered? <u>Don't Forget</u>: Keep detailed records, and use the **Sample Client Record** chart in the back of this book.

◇   *How permanent?* Regarding chemical processes to the hair, nothing is forever, but unlike hair color options of temporary, semi-permanent, demi-permanent, and permanent color, perming and relaxing boxed kits for home use *are* permanent until the hair is eventually cut off or chemically altered. Some natural reversal does occur, however--caused by hair continuing to restructure itself due to the environment (sun, wind, and water), and physical treatment (cleansing, conditioning, blowing, and brushing) taking its toll. Curls soften and straightened hair reverts just as colored hair fades or changes. You can minimize or maximize the lasting time of your perm or relaxer, but only an experienced professional knows which combination of tools and solutions need to be used for less or more permanency. <u>Tip</u>: Use tools and products which make the hair temporarily curly or straight before deciding to go more permanent at home.

◇   *Saving how much money?* Many people are astonished to discover that the actual cost for basic chemical solutions is much lower than the service price would suggest. But not only does your technician use several additional products in chemical preparation and completion, she is also skilled in practical application. Using clean partings, smoothing delicate hair ends (which can otherwise frizz and break), strategically and properly placing curling rods, and keeping a close eye on hair and scalp reactions are all part of achieving an optimal result. In a nutshell, a specialist's education in many areas of chemical work is sure to prove worthwhile.

Special note regarding touch-ups for perms and relaxers: Even professionals must be careful about overlapping chemicals. Touch-ups should concentrate on virgin outgrowth with only minimal exposure to pre-treated hair to avoid damage or breakage. In addition, professionals are skilled in using protective papers and wraps to avoid over-perming.

Did you know? A common misconception is that what you eat today will directly affect your hair or skin tomorrow. Diet, medication, and vitamins *can* have an effect on your hair and skin, but only if ingested over a period of time. How? Vitamins and a balanced diet will have a positive (if only subtle) effect on your hair and skin. Medications, and poor nutrition, on the other hand, can have an adverse effect on hair and skin and can interfere with chemical processes. Consult your doctor or pharmacist.

Most Common Problems With Perming/Relaxing At Home

Problem	Reason
odor	insufficient rinsing
over-processing	solution left on too long
under-processing	solution not left on long enough
skin irritation	solution left on hair, skin
uneven curl or straightness	uneven tension or application
very dry or frizzy hair	over-processing
early perm relaxation or relaxed hair reverting back to curl	insufficient neutralization
breakage	too much tension/ solution too strong for hair

AT-HOME TIPS FOR PERM/RELAXER RETENTION:

- Shampoo as little as possible. (Rinsing and conditioning are okay.)
- Condition with water soluble or suggested conditioners only.
- Don't expose treated hair to excessive blow-drying, curling, or setting.
- Use products to help. Examples include perm revitalizers, acid pH rinses for permed hair, cleansers and moisturizers designed for permed hair, and styling products that are water soluble and don't weigh the hair down.

Skin & Nails At Home

Aside from simple care such as cleansing and moisturizing the skin and do-it-yourself manicures with file and polish, skin and nail care that requires the use of special tools, chemicals or equipment should not be performed at home. Too much nail buffing or ridge smoothing, too many mud masks on the face, incorrect use of removers for unwanted hair, or over-use of acetone to remove artificial nails, can all cause damage to the skin and nails. Mistakes (such as chemical burns) resulting from incorrect use of solutions or procedures can have devastating and long-term---if not permanent--repercussions. And, since skin and nail beds cannot be cut off the way your hair can be, more care needs to be taken when applying chemicals directly to the skin to bring about a "permanent" change. For simple procedures, talk the idea through with an experienced skin care professional to get product information, detailed instructions, and advice.

If you must use at-home pharmaceutical products, chemicals, or even botanicals for the skin and nails, keep in mind the following:

◇ *Timing*. Whether it's an herbal facial mask, hair remover, or other product that requires timely removal, do not exceed the recommended time that the product is active on the skin or nails unless supervised by a professional.

◇ *Stopping the action*. When a chemical is to be stopped by either rinsing, cleansing, or neutralizing, it must be stopped immediately and completely to avoid over-processing. Follow all directions to the letter.

◇ **_Timely removal_**. Some at-home kits fail to stress the total removal of certain products, add-ons, or extensions at some point. These products--such as artificial nail extensions--might otherwise be left on the nails or skin indefinitely. Since each circumstance is different, a professional will be happy to assist you.

Tip: If you want to apply treatments at home, ask a skin care specialist to recommend or prescribe the right product or combination of products for you.

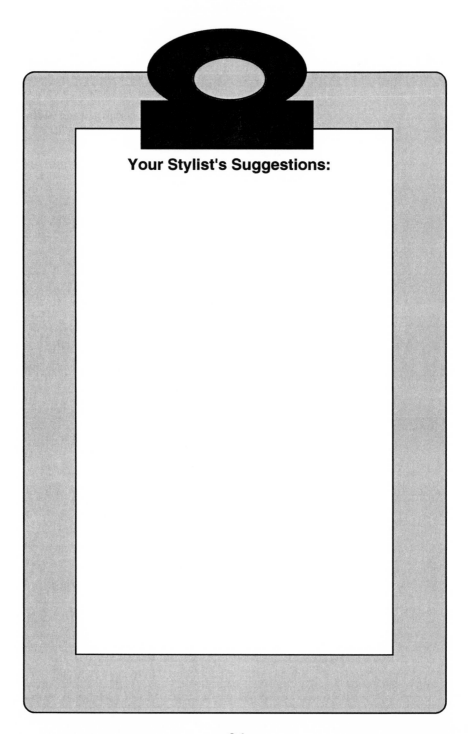

Your Stylist's Suggestions:

9

MORE STUFF

Salon & Spa Dangers

It would be inaccurate to say that the salon or spa environment is absolutely safe. Some clients *and* stylists have opted to stay away from the salon environment for fear of over-exposure to ammonias, tints, hair sprays, fumes, and so on. The good news is that very little evidence in a sea of research shows a direct link between the various products and chemicals used in the salon and the development of any serious condition or illness. In fact, when studies found a link between on-the-scalp, dark hair color dyes and cancer in laboratory animals several years ago, the dyes were replaced--even though the research was inconclusive. Furthermore, the majority of people who have frequented salons and used hair and skin care products all of their lives have had no related problems or illnesses whatsoever.

Those most at risk? Chemical technicians who work in the salons for years--inhaling and even accidentally ingesting chemicals on a daily basis. Clients who are allergy-prone or have respiratory problems could also become ill as a result of the salon or spa environment--particularly those environments that are not well-ventilated--so careful observation and regular medical check-ups are strongly advised. Concerned? Find out if your salon has a good air filtration system or opened windows. More good news? Sanitation and sterilization laws need to be strictly followed and salons are checked regularly by health inspectors. Wet sanitizers (disinfectants or alcohol) and dry sanitizers (active fumigants) for destroying bacteria must be used for salon tools and implements.

ALERT!! If you suspect that sanitation laws are not being observed in a salon, contact the public health office in your state.

The Myth: No Pain No Gain

Some salon and spa services are not entirely pain free. Some hair removal services, extractions of impurities during facials, or a rigorous foot sloughing of dead tissue during a pedicure may cause some discomfort. Tingling sensations from permanent waving solutions, and mild to moderate scalp pain from bleaching or hair relaxing are also common complaints. However, *NEVER* let a procedure that produces pain go unquestioned. In fact, let your stylist know even if you are experiencing slight pain. (Also see What You Must Always Tell Your Stylist in **COMMUNICATING WITH YOUR STYLIST**, p. 35.)

WARNING! No salon or spa treatment recommended in this guide should cause severe pain.

Regarding Pregnancy

The biggest concern here may have to do with colors or perms which are applied "on-the-scalp" or certain skin care products which penetrate or are absorbed by the skin. Some doctors will suggest that pregnant clients not have these types of services performed during the first trimester; some tell their clients to stay away from all chemical services for the entire pregnancy; and some doctors show little concern regarding most salon and spa services since it is doubtful that a fetus is affected by hair coloring, perming, relaxing, and most skin care treatments. Although many clients continue with on-the-scalp procedures, be sure to consult your doctor and together decide what is best. The safest techniques? Temporary or semi-permanent hair color, "off-the scalp" highlights, "wet" perms that don't require the use of chemicals, and non-penetrating skin care products.

Did you know? Many moms-to-be experience changes to their hair, skin, and nails during pregnancy and up to one year after the birth of their children. While pregnant, the changes may be positive or negative due to a woman's raging hormone levels. Fuller hair, better complexion, and stronger nails are sometimes visible, but when hormone levels are suppressed, hair loss, poor complexion, and weak and splitting nails are the most common negative side effects. Experiencing a problem? Talk with your stylist for optimal at-home maintenance and keep your doctor posted.

Wigs & Hair Pieces

Wigs are used much more frequently than people realize because--as with expert hair color and permanent waves--wigs today are so natural-looking that even a professional can't always tell without close inspection. The reason? Real, human hair is used for many of today's hair pieces, and the newest hair weaving techniques are so intricate that wig-making has become an art form. Hair replacement companies can even match your own hair's color and texture just by taking a few samples of your hair. Whether you need a piece permanently bonded to your own hair, a toupee that is removable, a partial piece or full head of hair, or clip-on temporary extensions, read the following tips before you begin your search.

◇ **Determine your need**. If you do some research, you'll discover there is a whole world out there for add-on hair whether you are seeking hair replacement with the help of a physician, camouflaging hair loss with a customized wig, or using a hair piece for adornment or simple change. What else is there? Thin strands of hair can either be braided into your own hair or glued on (with a liquid polymer) for length or more fullness. Depending on your needs and the artist's technique, these extensions can remain in the hair for months--with regular shampooing and finishing--while the natural hair continues to grow. Important: If you want permanent hair replacement, "plugs", or any other type of scalp-invading therapy, it is imperative that you seek out a physician who specializes in this area.

◇ **Let your fingers do the walking**. Scanning the yellow pages can supply you with an abundance of information. Need a wig for a costume? Don't go to a wig shop that sells the best wigs on the market where you will spend more money than necessary. Instead, buy a synthetic wig from a party store or costume shop. On the other hand, if you want the most natural-looking hair piece you can find, there are several companies that will customize a full wig or piece for you. You can even join a hair club for regular maintenance of your hair piece. For comb-in or clip-on extensions, a call to your local beauty supply store can lead you to the right place. F.Y.I: The amount of money you spend on a wig is almost always directly related to the quality of the product.

◇ ***Take your wig to the salon***. Establishments that sell customized hair pieces usually have a stylist on staff who will trim the piece for you while you wear it--usually included in the price. But as competent as these stylists are, you may encounter the same disappointment you would from going to a new stylist for the first time. Better? Let the establishment's stylist give it a trim first, and then take it to your regular stylist for a touch-up if necessary.

Did you know? A chemical technician who has experience working on wigs can also chemically alter your wig by adding some curl, highlights, or changing the entire color.

Hair, Skin & Ethnicity

On many levels, African-American, Hispanic, Asian, and Anglo-American clients each have unique salon needs. Not only do dark and light hair require opposite approaches to achieve certain hair colors and the use of different make-up colors to complement dark and light complexions, but the composition of the hair and skin actually *is* different among the races. In other words, clients belonging to a particular culture or race require salon staff to be proficient in dealing with their hair or skin's chemical composition, physical conditions, attributes, and limitations. All of these differences are important--not only to provide services for appearances sake--but to apply chemical treatments correctly. Without specialized knowledge of ethnic differences in hair and skin, results from improperly used products can be devastating. Obviously, there are many salon and spa services that do not require a different approach because of race, but just as colorists specialize in coloring and massage therapists are skilled in healing touch, seeing someone who is familiar with *your* hair and skin type makes good sense. <u>Note</u>: What is important is not the ethnicity of the stylist, but the experience she has with a diverse or multi-cultural clientele. If you're not familiar with your stylist's clientele, ask the stylist or receptionist.

Tips While Traveling

◇ ***Get a referral.*** Walking into just any salon off the street in a strange city or country is asking for trouble. If there is no one to ask, use the tips in The Right Salon For You in **SALONS** on p. 55. And if staying in a hotel, ask the concierge.

◇ ***Mind the language barriers.*** In a foreign land you may get a nod in reply to your request, but unless your stylist can repeat back what you're asking for, don't assume you've been understood. Even in English-speaking countries, word choice and sentence structure can make getting your point across as impossible as if you are speaking different languages. <u>Hint</u>: Have a couple of key phrases or words written down in the language spoken where you're visiting.

◇ ***Use every trick in the book.*** You may never find a better time to review the tips suggested in **COMMUNICATING WITH YOUR STYLIST** (beginning on p. 26) than when seeing a stylist for the first time while on the road. Although you're planning to return to your home stylist, even a one-time disaster can set you back or alter your goals.

◇ ***Keep it simple.*** The best way to head off a disappointment while far from home is to not put yourself in a position to deal with anything long-term. Just think *temporary* regarding chemical treatment, and *trims* regarding haircuts. The best kind of salon services while traveling? File & polish manicures and pedicures, make-up applications, basic table or seated massages, and hair styling.

Did you know? Hotel and resort stylists are typically very skilled in the areas of one-time service. Why? Hair styling for special occasions, nail, and spa services are the services that hotel and resort guests take advantage of the most-- providing those stylists with ample experience.

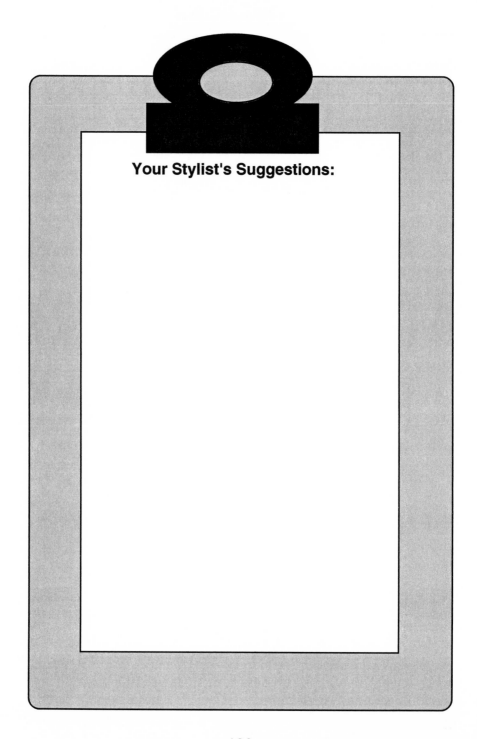

Your Stylist's Suggestions:

Sample Client Record

Date	Hair or Skin's Present Condition	Technique, Formula, or Procedure	Results	Care & Maintenance	Goal